THE POST OFFICE OF INDIA

THE POST OFFICE OF INDIA AND ITS STORY

GEOFFREY CLARKE

GYAN

Published by

GYAN

Gyan Publishing House
5, Ansari Road
Daryaganj, New Delhi-110002
Phone: 011-47034999, 9811692060
E-mail: books@gyanbooks.com

Distribution Network
gyanbooks.com
India, USA, Canada, UK, Australia, France

ISBN : 978-81-212-9182-8 (PB)
First Published, 1921

2nd Impression 2023

Printed at: Gyan Press, Delhi.

THE POST OFFICE OF INDIA
Author: GEOFFREY CLARKE

THE POST OFFICE OF INDIA

GROUP OF SENIOR OFFICERS OF THE POST OFFICE IN 1884

P. SHERIDAN, H. M. KISCH, F. C. O'BRIEN, E. R. DOUGLAS, W. ALPIN, J. DILLON, W. J. HAM, F. E. HOGG (*Director General*), G. J. HYNES, H. L. M. JAMES, RAI BAHADUR SUNDER LAL, E. HUTTON

THE POST OFFICE OF INDIA AND ITS STORY

BY GEOFFREY CLARKE
INDIAN CIVIL SERVICE

WITH SIXTEEN ILLUSTRATIONS

LONDON : JOHN LANE THE BODLEY HEAD
NEW YORK : JOHN LANE COMPANY MCMXXI

PREFACE

WHEN I first decided to write a short account of the Post Office of India my intention was to close my story with the amalgamation of the Post Office and the Telegraph Department, which took place in 1913. Publication has been delayed for various reasons, chiefly owing to the outbreak of the war in 1914, and since then many strange things have happened. Consequently I have had to revise several chapters and felt compelled to write one upon the wonderful work done by the Indian Post Office in the Great War. I have also brought the statistical information up to the year 1918. Much of the matter referring to the early posts in India has already been given in Mr. Hamilton's book, *An Outline of Postal History and Practice*. This is only natural, as we have both drawn from the same sources—namely, the records of the Postal Directorate in Calcutta. I have tried to tell the story of the Post Office in such a way as to be interesting to the general reader as well as useful to the student. The ordinary routine of post office work is not exciting, but the effect of the work, the benefits it confers, the dependence of the public upon its proper execution, are themes to inspire the pen of a romantic writer. "The Romance of the Post Office" was the title of a delightful article in

Blackwood's Magazine by Sir Arthur Fanshawe, late Director-General of the Department, and to this article I must acknowledge my obligations for several passages in the book.

I am much indebted to Mr. R. W. Hanson and Mr. F. F. Shout, Assistant Directors-General of the Post Office of India, for their assistance in producing this work. Mr. Hanson is responsible for the chapter on "The Post Office in Mesopotamia and the Persian Gulf," and Mr. Shout for the chapter on "The Sea Post Office" and the paragraphs dealing with the District Post, as well as for the Index.

The chapter upon Indian stamps is based largely upon *The Postage and Telegraph Stamps of British India*, by Hausburg, Stewart-Wilson and Crofton, published by Messrs. Stanley Gibbons, and I am greatly indebted to Messrs. Stanley Gibbons for the loan of their blocks and for permission to use them in this book.

CONTENTS

APPENDICES

ILLUSTRATIONS

THE POST OFFICE OF INDIA

THE POST OFFICE OF INDIA : : AND ITS STORY : :

CHAPTER I

THE POST OFFICE OF INDIA

TO anyone connected with the work of the Post Office of India it is almost inconceivable that the present institution, with its vast organization and its elaborate system, has grown up in the course of little more than half a century. Previous to 1854 the Post Office was a medley of services in different provinces, each having separate rules and different rates of postage. Regular mails were conveyed over a very few main lines between important towns, and Collectors of districts were responsible for the management of their own local post offices. There were no postage stamps, and since rates were levied according to distance, and distances were often unknown, the position of a postal clerk in a large office was a distinctly lucrative one. In large cantonments a military officer with plenty of other duties was usually postmaster, and his supervision was at best sketchy, especially during the snipe shooting season.

In 1850 a Commission of the kind with which we are

now so familiar both in India and England was appointed to consider the state of the postal services, and the result of its deliberations was the Post Office Act of 1854 and the conversion of the Post Office into an Imperial Department under a single head called the Director-General. Uniform rates of postage were introduced and postage stamps instead of cash payments were brought into use. That marvellous set of rules known as the Post Office Manual was prepared, which has since grown into four healthy volumes. Every Official in the Department is supposed to have the contents of these at his fingers' ends, but in reality few have ever read them through, and anyone who attempted to obey all their instructions would find himself sadly hampered in the exercise of his duties. The appointment of a Director-General, by bringing the separate services under a single administration, laid the foundation for future progress. Suitable officers were recruited and were taught their duties, better pay and improved prospects of promotion were a great inducement to the staff to take an interest in the work, and through communications which took no account of district or provincial boundaries were established.

The gradual growth of the powers of the Director-General has largely depended on the needs of the Department, and also, to an appreciable extent, upon his own strength of will and his personal relations with the Member of Council, who controls the Department of Government to which the Post Office is subordinate.[1] The Director-General is assisted by two Deputy Directors, who are, in fact, the Secretaries of the Post Office, and under these again are four Assistant Directors

[1] This is at present the Department of Commerce.

in charge of four main branches of Post Office work. All the above officers have the title " General " attached to their designations in order to increase their self-respect, but I have omitted it to avoid an annoying reiteration. Of the three personal assistants, one has to be a walking encyclopædia since he is in personal attendance on the Director-General ; the others are financial and technical experts. The office itself is under the immediate supervision of a titled Bengalee gentleman of considerable attainments, and his clerks are mostly Bengalee graduates whose abilities are supposed to vary with their salaries.

For the purposes of administration, thc whole of India and Burma is divided into eight circles, corresponding with Presidencies and Provinces as far as possible. Each of these is under the control of a Postmaster-General, who is sometimes a member of the Indian Civil Service and sometimes an official of the Department. The powers of a Postmaster-General are great, his patronage is large and the working of the Post Office is dependent on his capacity for railway travelling at all seasons of the year. His circle is divided into divisions in charge of Superintendents, who should be little understudies of himself.

The real business of the Department, however, is performed by post offices, and these are divided into head, sub and branch offices. The head office is the account and controlling office of one or more districts and is in charge of a postmaster, who in large towns ranks as a divisional officer. The sub-office is under the control of a head office for account purposes. It does all kinds of postal work and is always opened where there is a sufficiency of correspondence to justify its existence. The branch office is only intended for villages and places where there is no need of a sub-office. It is really the pioneer of the Department for the purpose of opening up new areas to postal communications. In small places a branch office is put in charge of a schoolmaster, a shop-keeper or any other local resident who has sufficient education to keep the very simple accounts required, and by this means the Post Office is able to give the advantages of its great organization to villages which could never support a departmental office. A still cheaper agency is used for the outlying hamlets, which only receive and send a few letters a week. These are visited periodically by the village or rural postman, who is a kind of perambulating branch office. He delivers letters and money orders, and also receives articles for despatch. He sells stamps and quinine, and being a local man he has to face a certain amount of public opinion if he doesn't act fair and square towards the villagers in his beat. In some hill tracts he is provided with a bugle to announce his arrival, and to the inhabitants of these he brings news of the outside world; he writes their letters and explains to them his own conception of the mysteries of the money order system.

But what would be the use of all these offices and all this organization without lines of communication? The chief lines are, of course, the railways, but they form a separate organization and will be discussed in another chapter. For places off the railway there are motor lines and tonga services, such as that sung by Kipling between Kalka and Simla but now a thing of the past owing to the completion of the hill railway. The romance of the Post Office, however, must always lie in the mail runner, or hirkara as he is called in old books on India. The number of tigers sated with his flesh is past count, the Himalayan snows have overwhelmed him, flooded rivers have carried him off and oozy swamps sucked him down. But in the face of all these dangers, has the runner ever failed to do his duty? According to the stories, never, and in real life perhaps not more than once or twice.

> Is the torrent in spate? He must ford it or swim.
> Has the rain wrecked the road? He must climb by the cliff.
> The service admits not a but, nor an if,
> While the breath's in his mouth, he must bear without fail
> In the name of the Emperor—the "Overland Mail."—KIPLING.

Postal runners are largely drawn from the less civilized races of India, many of whom are animists by religion. They will face wild beasts and wandering criminals, but will go miles to avoid an evil spirit in a tree. With them the mail bag is a kind of fetish which must be protected and got to its destination at all costs. Dishonesty among them is almost unknown and they are wonderfully true to their salt, which with them seldom exceeds twelve rupees a month. To prove that the old stories are not all myths, a case came before the Director-General recently in a rather peculiar manner. The Audit Office, that soulless machine which drives executive officers out of their minds, sent in an objection to a gratuity being given to the family of a runner who, when carrying the mails, had been eaten by a tiger. The objection was that gratuities were only given for death in special circumstances, for instance, when death occurred in the performance of some specially courageous action, and that, since carrying the mails was part of the man's ordinary duty, his family was not entitled to any consideration. The actual story of the runner's death, as told by the villagers and the village watchman, is this: The runner's beat had been recently frequented by a man-eating tiger, and several of the country people had been carried off by him during the previous few days. On the afternoon in question the tiger was known to be in the neighbourhood, and when the mails arrived the villagers warned the runner not to go then, but to wait until next morning. Since the man-eater was an early feeder—that is to say, he killed his prey early in the afternoon, the runner waited until five o'clock and then persuaded the village watchman to accompany him. He hadn't gone more than two miles when out came the tiger and seized him. The watchman escaped and took the mails to the next stage, and the family of the man who nobly faced death in the execution of his duty was deprived of its wage-earner. This is a very bald account of a really heroic deed, and it is pleasing to learn that Mr. Levett Yeats, the Accountant-General of the Post Office at the time, who was the very soul of romance and chivalry, dealt with his objecting subordinate in a manner worthy of the heinous nature of his offence.

The road establishment of the Indian Post Office amounted to 18,160 persons out of a total staff of 108,324 on the 31st March, 1918, so there is some excuse for having devoted so much space to it. The postal staff had to deal with over 1200 millions of articles during the year, of which, according to the Annual Report of 1917–18, only ·22 per cent failed to reach their proper destination. When one considers that there are more than twenty written languages in India in common use, and that a large number of addresses are almost illegible and are mixed up with invocations to the Deity and many other high-sounding phrases, one can only say, "Bravo, the Post Office! How do you do it?" With such a large correspondence a handsome revenue might be expected, even when the minimum rate for letters is a halfpenny; but the Indian is a frugal person and he does most of his correspondence on farthing postcards, on which he can cram a great deal of information by carefully using every available portion. Postcards were introduced in 1879 and now account for nearly half of the articles handled. The private card, with a figure of some favourite god or goddess, is competing strongly with the ordinary Government postcard, and wonderful ingenuity is employed to enable the writer to avail himself of more space than the regulations permit. The unpaid letter is also much in evidence in India. There is an idea that a letter on which postage has to be collected is much more certain to reach its destination than a prepaid one. This heretical doctrine has been strongly condemned in several pamphlets issued by the Director-General, but with little effect. And who knows? Perhaps there is a certain amount of truth in it, founded on bitter experience. Unpaid postcards had to be abolished recently, when it was discovered that they were universally read and then returned to the postmen as refused. The writer generally concealed his identity from the officials, with the result that it was useless to try and recover the postage due.

Among a suspicious and ignorant people any innovation is likely to be looked at askance, and this is especially the case in India, where the introduction of postcards was received with suspicion, although their low price ensured a ready sale. An extract from the *Amrita Bazar Patrika*, one of the foremost Indian papers, shows that they were not at first regarded as an unmixed blessing. The extract is taken from the issue of the 18th July, 1879, and is as follows :—

"Postal cards are now a rage all over India. There are men who, to make the contents of the cards unintelligible, make them altogether illegible. Some express themselves in hints which are not only unintelligible to the postal clerk and peon, but to the person addressed also. Others have got a notion that all letters, to be sent either through the Post or through private harkaras, must be written on postcards, that being the hookum[1] of the Sirkar; and it is not unusual to see a fat and ignorant, though extremely loyal and law-abiding, zemindar[2] sending his letters to his steward written on half a score of postcards, one or two not sufficing to contain his great thoughts. There are others who write their thoughts on postcards and enclose them in an envelope, and attach a half-anna stamp before posting. These men have naturally raised a loud complaint against the unconscionable exactions of Government, and native papers given to writing sedition should not let slip this opportunity of indulging their profitable pastime. But the great difficulty is to teach the people on which side of the card the address is to be written, and we think it will be some years before they are enlightened in this respect. But really does it matter much if the address is written on the wrong side? We think that the people of India living under the enlightened rule of the British should have the privilege of writing the address on whichever side they like."

What a merry time the poor sorters would have if the sentiments expressed in the last sentence were given

[1] Order. [2] Landholder.

effect to! But doubtless the *Amrita Bazar Patrika*, with its enlightened staff, its splendid circulation and carefully printed addresses would scarcely maintain the same opinions now.

The Post Office of India must be congratulated upon its good fortune in never having been regarded by Government as a revenue-producing Department, and as long as it paid its way with a small surplus the Powers were satisfied. Any excess was devoted to improvements in the service, and full advantage has been given to this concession in past years by the introduction of many reforms destined to meet the growing needs of the country. Recently, postage rates were reduced to such an extent that for a few years the Post Office worked at a loss, a most unsatisfactory state of affairs; however, a marked recovery is noticeable already and it is again a self-supporting institution, the gross revenue for the year ending the 31st March, 1918, being more than 416 lakhs[1] of rupees, which gave a net surplus of nearly 50 lakhs on the year's working.

From being merely an agency for the conveyance and distribution of letters and light articles, the Post Office has gradually undertaken an enormous amount of what may be called non-postal work. It deals with vast numbers of money orders, collects the price of goods for tradesmen, pays pensioners, sells quinine, deals in Government loans, and is the poor man's bank, all of which matters will be dealt with separately. It is to be hoped that no new line of business is going to be taken up in the near future, such as the sale of railway tickets, which was once seriously proposed, or else the principal duty of the Department may be forgotten in the turmoil of the side shows.

[1] One lakh = Rs. 100,000.

CHAPTER II

THE ORIGIN OF THE POST OFFICE

THE Postal System of India, like that of other countries, had its origin in the necessity of maintaining communication throughout the various parts of a great Empire in order that the Emperor might be kept continuously informed of what was taking place and might be able to keep in constant touch with the officers in charge of Provinces at a distance from the Capital. When Ibn Batuta was travelling in India in the middle of the fourteenth century he found an organized system of couriers established throughout the country governed at that time by the great Mahomed Din Tughlak. The system seems to have been very similar to that which existed in the Roman Empire, and is thus described :

" There are in Hindustan two kinds of couriers, horse and foot ; these they generally term ' El Wolak.' The horse-courier, which is generally part of the Sultan's cavalry, is stationed at a distance of every four miles. As to the foot-couriers there will be one at the distance of every mile occupying stations which they call ' El Davah " and making on the whole three miles ; so that there is, at the distance of every three miles, an inhabited village, and without this, three sentry boxes where the couriers sit prepared for motion with their loins girded. In the hands of each is a whip about two cubits long, and upon the head of this are small bells. Whenever, therefore, one of the couriers leaves any city he takes his despatches in one hand and the whip, which he keeps constantly shaking, in the other. In this manner he proceeds to the nearest foot-courier and, as he approaches, shakes his whip. Upon this out comes another who takes the despatches and so proceeds to the next. For this reason it is that the Sultan receives his despatches in so short a time."

Some of the oldest runners' lines in India were established for the purpose of conveying fruit and flowers to famous temples, and Colonel Broughton in his most interesting book, *Letters from a Mahratta Camp*, describes one such line between Udeypore and Pushkar in Rajputana. In his *Historical Sketches of the South of India*, Colonel Wilks tells us that among the earliest measures of Raja Chick Deo Raj of Mysore, who came to the throne in 1672, was the establishment of a regular post throughout his dominions. The Post Office in Mysore was not merely an ordinary instrument for conveying intelligence, but an extraordinary one for obtaining it. The postmasters were confidential agents of the Court and the inferior servants were professed spies, who made regular reports of the secret transactions of the districts in which they were stationed. This system, which was more fully developed by Hyder Ali, became a terrible instrument of despotism. The Moghul Emperors kept up a regular system of daks, and Ferishta tells us that Sher Shah, during his short reign of five years, 1541–1545, was the first who ever employed a mounted post in India. He constructed a road from Sonarung in Bengal to the banks of the Indus in Sind, a distance of two thousand miles, and placed two horses on the road at every two miles. The Emperor Akbar had post houses built at stages ten miles apart on the principal roads and swift Turki horses were placed at each stage. One of these post houses can still be seen on the road between Agra and Sikandra.

The British do not appear to have found any established system of communication when they began to extend their dominion in India, and in the beginning of the eighteenth century it was a matter of no small difficulty to send a letter more than a distance of one hundred miles. A regular postal system was first introduced by Lord Clive in 1766, and the zemindars or landholders along the various routes were held responsible for the supply of runners to carry the mails. For this service a deduction was made in their rents in proportion to the number of runners supplied. The order recorded in the Minutes of Consultations of the 24th March is as follows :—

"For the Better Regulation of Dauks"

"Ordered that in future all letters be despatched from the Government House; the postmaster or his assistant attending every night to sort and see them sent off; that the letters to the different Inland Settlements be made up in separate bags, sealed with the Company's seal; that none may open the packets except the Chiefs at the different places, who are to open only their own respective packets; and

"Ordered that they be directed to observe the same rule with respect to the letters sent down to Calcutta."

The following is an extract from the Public Proceedings 7th July, 1766 :—

"As there have been of late frequent miscarriages of packets to and from Madras without possibility of tracing the cause, not knowing the stages where they do happen, as no advice is ever sent us by the neighbouring Residencies, and as this on any emergency may be attended with the worst of consequences, it is agreed to establish the following Rules and communicate them to the Presidency of Madras, recommending the same to be circulated to the factories and Residencies subordinate to them, as we shall do to those dependent on Bengal:—

"That the packets henceforward be numbered in regular succession for the present season from this time to the end of the year, and in future from the 1st January to the last of December.

"That the day and hour of despatch as well as the number be noted on the tickets affixed to the packets; that on every packet the number and date of the next preceding despatch be noted.

"That in order to have the earliest information of the loss of a packet at any time, the Resident or Chief of a factory shall regularly give advice of the receipt of each packet to the Resident of the stage from whence it came last.

"That when any packets are found to be missing the Chiefs or Residents at the two nearest stages shall immediately make it their business to examine the Dauks or Tappies very particularly, and punish them severely when they do not give a satisfactory account how the packets came to be lost, giving advice in the meantime to each Presidency.

"That the Postmaster at Calcutta and Residents at

Balasore, Cuttack and Ganjam do keep separate registers of despatches to and from Madras.

"That all packets be sealed with the Governor's as well as the Company's seal to prevent their being opened till they arrive at the destined place.

"And as we have reason to believe that by proper attention to the Tappies, the communication with Madras may be more expeditious, particularly between Vizagapatam and Bandermalanka, where making allowances for passing the Rivers, it is remarked they are very tardy, it is agreed to write to the gentlemen at Madras to mention this to their subordinate factories that they may fall upon proper measures to remedy it, and recommending small boats or saugarees to be stationed at the different rivers."

Under the administration of Warren Hastings the Post Office in India was placed on a better footing and steps were taken to make the posts which were established for official purposes more generally available for private communications. In January, 1774, the details of a regular system were laid down, which was brought into force on the 31st March, 1774. A Postmaster-General was appointed and postage was charged for the first time on private letters. The lowest rate of letter postage was two annas per hundred miles, and copper tickets of the value of two annas, to be used solely for postal purposes, were specially struck for public convenience.

In November, 1784, revised regulations for the Post Office were laid down which took effect in the province of Bengal from December of that year. In 1785 Madras followed suit upon proposals made by Mr. J. P. Burlton, a junior civilian in Government service. He suggested the adoption of a regular postal system on the lines of Bengal, under which all letters except those on the public service should pay postage. In 1786 Mr. Archibald Campbell was made Postmaster-General, Madras, and arrangements were made for fortnightly services to Calcutta and Bombay. There was some dispute between the Court of Directors and the Madras Government regarding the appointment of a Postmaster-General. The former refused to accept Mr. Campbell and nominated Mr. Burlton; the latter objected to Mr. Burlton and appointed Mr. Legge Wilks, who was shortly afterwards succeeded by Mr. Oliver Colt.

For the next fifty years the history of the Post Office is obscure. The territory occupied by the East India Company in 1784 consisted of three isolated portions adjoining the three presidency towns of Calcutta, Madras and Bombay. The Company obtained the administrative control of part of the Carnatic and the provinces known as the Northern Circars in 1761. The fiscal administration of the provinces of Bengal, Behar and Orissa was handed over by the Delhi Emperor in 1765, and by the Treaty of Salbai in 1782 the Bombay Government retained the islands of Elephanta and Salsette.

In 1798 Lord Wellesley arrived in India inspired by Imperial projects which were destined to change the map of the country. In 1799 Tippoo, Sultan of Mysore, was defeated and slain at Seringapatam, and the Carnatic or south-eastern portion of India ruled by the Nawab of Arcot, as well as the principality of Tanjore, were placed under British rule. These territories constitute the greater part of the present Madras Presidency. In 1801 the whole of the tract between the Ganges and Jumna, known as the Doab, with Rohilkhand, were obtained by purchase from the Nawab Vizir of Oudh. In 1803, after the second Mahratta War, Orissa was forfeited to the British and Berar to the Nizam of Hyderabad. In 1815 the Himalayan States were taken from the Nepalese, in 1817 the Pindaris were crushed in Central India and in 1818, after the third Mahratta War, the Bombay Presidency was formed. Assam was annexed in 1826, and Bharatpur taken in 1827.

The extension of postal services over this vast increase of territory can be traced only by scattered references in official documents. There was no general postal system in the country prior to 1837. A few main lines of couriers connecting the principal towns in the various provinces with the seat of Government had been established for the conveyance of Government letters and parcels, but the use of these mail services by private persons was conceded only as a privilege. The local posts in districts between police stations and head-quarters were maintained by the zemindars or landholders of each district, and their duties in this respect are laid down in Bengal Regulation XX of 1817. The postmasters of Presidency towns exercised the functions of a Postmaster-General in their own provinces up to 1785, and the Collectors or district officers were responsible for post office and mail lines within the limits of their own jurisdictions. There was no central authority to secure the co-operation of postal officials in different provinces or to maintain uniformity of procedure, and the charges for the conveyance of letters, which, in the absence of postage stamps, were levied in cash, varied according to weight and distance. Thus the cost of conveyance of a letter from Calcutta to Bombay was one rupee a tola ($\frac{2}{5}$ oz. approximately), and from Calcutta to Agra twelve annas a tola. As postal officials were inclined to get as much as possible out of the public, private posts existed everywhere and were able to compete successfully with the Government services.

The letters of Victor Jacquemont, who travelled in India in 1830 as Naturalist to the Royal Museum of Natural History, Paris, throw some light on the working of the Post Office at the time. The post was carried altogether by runners, and the travellers' bungalows on the various routes were under the Post Office. According to Jacquemont, three servants were attached by the postal administration to each bungalow, to look after the comforts of travellers and to supply them with palanquin bearers. Letters seem to have had very uncertain careers. The usual time from France to Upper India was eight months. Jacquemont had no great faith in the post. On several occasions he trusts his letters to the Almighty to watch over during their travels.

Under the provisions of Act XVII of 1837 a public post was established and Government assumed the exclusive right to convey letters for hire in the territories of the East India Company. Uniformity was attempted by the issue to all post offices of elaborate polymetrical tables, which fixed the charges to be levied on the principal routes. The Act of 1837 caused a great deal of dissatisfaction owing to the abolition of many private and well-organized services which were not at once replaced, or else replaced very inefficiently, by Government services. The landholders had to pay a local cess to maintain the District Posts, and they felt it a distinct grievance that they should have to pay for the upkeep of these, as well as fees for their correspondence, while all official letters were carried free of charge. An inquiry made by Captain Taylor of the Bengal Establishment into the working of the 1837 Act brought many of these grievances to light, and on his recommendation certain improvements were made in the interests of the landholders. Thus there grew up in India a dual system of posts—on the one hand, the Imperial Post, which controlled all main routes and large offices ; on the other, the District Post, which was entirely local and controlled the rural services in each district. The establishments were quite separate, and where the two systems came in contact there was often a great deal of friction.

The principle on which the District Post was based was the liability of landholders to maintain communications for Government purposes between the executive head of a district and his subordinates in outlying places —a responsibility which in many instances they were glad to discharge by a money payment to the magistrate who undertook the organization of the requisite agency. The laws under which it was administered were framed with the object of levying a small cess in each district. This was used, at the discretion of the magistrate, for the payment of dak-runners and other persons who conveyed correspondence between police stations and district officials. This local post undoubtedly existed from ancient times, and its maintenance was a liability to which the landholders had been subject from a period long before the advent of British rule.

The District Post in India, which was an important, though not very efficient, auxiliary to the Imperial Post, thus owed its origin to the need for maintaining the means of official communication between the headquarters of each district and the revenue and police stations in the interior, where the general wants of the locality were not such as to call for the provision of

Imperial post offices. It consisted of lines of communication connecting such stations, and was maintained primarily for the conveyance of official correspondence in accordance with the requirements of each district, but subsequently it was also made available for private correspondence.

In some parts of the country the cost of the District Post lines was met by local cesses specially levied for the purpose, and in other places it was met from Imperial or provincial grants as a charge on the general revenues of the country.

Originally the District Post in India was managed by district officers or other local officials quite independently of the Imperial Post, but, in order to increase the efficiency of the service, Local Governments and Administrations were asked to transfer the management to the officers of the Imperial Post Office. The North-Western Provinces (now United Provinces) Government was the first to accept the proposal, and the management of the District Post there was taken over by the Postmaster-General of the circle in the year 1864. This arrangement did not constitute an incorporation of the District Post with the Imperial Post, but merely a transfer of the management of the former to the officers of the latter, the financial control of the District Post remaining as before with the Local Government. As was anticipated, this measure led to rapid development of private correspondence, an acceleration of the speed at which the mails were carried and a marked improvement in the postal arrangements in the interior of districts. Consequently the objections which were at first raised in many quarters were silenced, and the other Local Governments and Administrations soon fell into line, so that in the course of the next fourteen years the management of the whole of the District Post throughout India was gradually transferred to the Imperial Post Office.

As the number of Imperial post offices increased the primary object of the District Post became less important and its funds were devoted more and more to the extension of rural delivery and postal facilities in backward rural tracts. As these tracts developed and the postal traffic produced sufficient revenue to cover the expenditure the Imperial Post took them over, and the money thus set free was used to start offices, lines and rural messengers in country not yet opened. In this way the District Post acted the part of pioneer to the Imperial Post and greatly assisted its progress.

In 1903, in connection with the revision of the Provincial Settlements, the Government of India decided to abolish the exceptional arrangement under which, in some provinces, a portion of the revenue and expenditure in connection with the District Post was included in the Provincial accounts. It was ordered that from the commencement of the new settlements all such receipts and charges which were then Provincial would be made Imperial. In accordance with this decision all the District Post establishments in the Presidencies of Bengal and Madras and the Province of Assam, which were formerly paid from Provincial funds, were brought directly on the general establishment of the Imperial Post Office with effect from the 1st April, 1904. Two years later the Government of India decided to take over the remaining District Post charges in India, and the District Post was abolished entirely with effect from the 1st April, 1906. It was at the same time ordered that from that date every postal charge would be an Imperial one and that no postal charges of any description whatsoever might be incurred from Provincial or Local funds.

In 1850 three Commissioners, Messrs. Courtney, Forbes and Beadon, were appointed by the Government of India to inquire into the methods for making the Post Office more efficient and more conducive to the convenience of the public than it had been hitherto.

In 1851 the Commissioners, after making exhaustive inquiries, presented a report which dealt with every phase of Post Office work, and on this report has been based the whole fabric of the present administration. The most important questions discussed were :

(1) The necessity for a uniform rate of postage irrespective of distance.
(2) The need for prepayment of postage by means of adhesive postage stamps.
(3) The fixing of a low initial rate of postage.
(4) The abolition of franking.
(5) The formation of the Post Office as an Imperial Department under a Director-General, with Postmasters-General in each province who would not be subject to the authority of the Local Government.
(6) The publication of Manual Rules for the use of postal officials.
(7) The establishment of sorting offices at suitable places.
(8) The introduction of money orders.
(9) The regulation of the Bhangy or Parcel Post.
(10) The introduction of cheap and uniform postage for newspapers, books, pamphlets, etc.
(11) The transfer of District Posts to the Imperial Post Office.

The report of the Commissioners is contained in a bulky volume of some six hundred pages, of which the preamble is most interesting and throws a great deal of light on the domestic history of India in the first half of the nineteenth century. The reforms are based throughout on the principle that the Post Office is to be maintained for the benefit of the people of India and not for the purposes of swelling the revenues, and it is greatly to the credit of the Government of India that in all times of stress and strain, as well as in times of prosperity, they have loyally observed this principle, although there have been many temptations to act contrary to it.

With the advance of postal administration in India in the last sixty years we can hardly realize the difficulties that had to be faced in 1851. One of the chief ones was the poverty of the great bulk of the population, many of whom could ill afford to spend even the smallest Indian coin, namely, one pie, a twelfth part of a penny, on anything that was not necessary for their own sustenance.

In dealing with this matter the following remarks of the Commissioners are very interesting :—

" In considering what plan of postage is best suited to the circumstances of India, and most likely to conduce to the convenience of the public, the social and commercial advancement of the country, and the ultimate financial advantage of the department, the difference between the circumstances of the European and native portion of the community must be distinctly borne in mind. It must be remembered that the former are very few in number, but, generally speaking, well educated and in affluent circumstances ; that they are accustomed and inclined to social correspondence, for which, from being collected at particular stations throughout the country, they have great facilities; and are comparatively little hindered from indulging in it by the expense which it entails on them, being for the most part regardless of the pecuniary advantage which they might derive from a more careful attention to the weight of their letters. The natives, on the other hand, are incalculably more numerous than their European fellow-subjects. Upon the moderate assumption that there are two thousand natives for every European, and that not more than 1 per cent of the former can read and write, still there must be twenty natives for every European who can correspond by the post without assistance, provided that the means of paying postage are within their reach, and that the receipt and delivery of their letters are facilitated. But they are poor, and, though well inclined to correspond, greatly prevented from doing so by the present high rates of postage to distant stations, and still more by the distance which separates the mass of them from the nearest post office, and by the consequent trouble, expense, uncertainty and perhaps loss, which the receipt and despatch of their letters involve. The occupations in which large numbers of natives are engaged connected with the internal trade of the country are such as naturally to render their correspondence on matters of business far more extensive than that of Europeans, the greater part of the latter being engaged in the service of Government and not under the necessity of writing letters except on their own personal concerns or those of their friends. With the improvement of the means of communication, extension of trade and the gradual spread of knowledge throughout the country, the instructed and writing portion of the native community will continue to bear an increasing ratio both to the rest of their fellow-country-men and to the European residents in India, but to the bulk even of these the amount they can afford to expend on the postage of their letters must ever be a matter of strict economical calculation. It may be regarded as certain that the utmost care will always be observed by the native community in keeping the weight of their letters within the minimum chargeable weight; and unless some considerable reduction is made in the existing rates of postage to distant places they will continue to resort to ingenious contrivances for the purpose of saving expenditure under that head, or avoiding it altogether."

The practice of "clubbing" or of enclosing a number of small letters in one cover addressed to a person who undertook to deliver them by hand was very common in India before 1850 and is not unknown at the present time. When the difference in cost between a single and double letter was considerable, this practice entailed a great loss of revenue to the Post Office, and in order to stop it the Commissioners proposed to make the unit of weight a quarter of a tola and to charge extra postage for each quarter tola of weight. The unit finally adopted was half a tola, as it was thought that Post Office clerks would have difficulty in detecting such small divisions of weight as a quarter of a tola. At the same time heavy penalties were imposed on clubbing, and the practice has gradually fallen into disuse.

Uniformity of postage irrespective of distance had many opponents at the time. It was recommended by the Commissioners on the ground of fairness, simplicity and the facilities it gave for the introduction of other improvements into the department. To use their own words: "Combined with a low rate of charge, it forms

SIR CHARLES STEWART WILSON, K.C.I.E.
DIRECTOR GENERAL 1906—1913

the conspicuous and chief benefit which the monopoly of the carriage of letters enables Government to confer upon the whole body of its subjects, by almost annihilating distance and placing it within the power of every individual to communicate freely with all parts of the Empire. It makes the Post Office what under any other system it never can be—the unrestricted means of diffusing knowledge, extending commerce and promoting in every way the social and intellectual improvement of the people. It is no longer an experiment, having been introduced with eminent success into the United Kingdom as well as into the United States of America, France, Spain and Russia."

There was a strong body of opinion in favour of the compulsory prepayment of postage in all cases on the ground that in India it was most difficult to collect the postage due on bearing letters; in fact, the letters were usually sent open, read by the addresses and then refused, so that both the sender and recipient got all they wanted out of the Post Office for nothing. However, wiser counsels prevailed. It was recognized that compulsory prepayment might mean great hardship in many cases, and the English system of charging double postage on unpaid articles was adopted.

These few extracts are sufficient to show the fine spirit that pervaded the work of the Commissioners. They were true Imperialists and never took the petty view, but adhered to the maxim of the greatest benefit to the greatest number. Their names are forgotten, but the result of their labours has remained in the fine organization now known as the Post Office of India.

CHAPTER III

EARLY POSTAL REGULATIONS

ACT XVII of 1837, the earliest enactment establishing a proper postal system in India, repealed Bombay Regulation XI of 1830 which declared all private dawks within the Bombay Presidency to be illegal. It conferred the exclusive right of carrying post for hire on the Governor-General in Council and fixed the penalty for evasion of this order at Rs.50 for each letter. The Bhangy Post was opened to the public with the condition that letters exceeding 12 tolas must be sent by bhangy wherever such a line existed. The Governor-General in Council was authorized to frame a scale of distances, according to which the rates for inland postage should be calculated and also to fix the rates for steamer and ship postage. Strict regulations were laid down compelling commanders of vessels to deliver all letters on board to the post office at each port of call, also to receive all letters handed over to them by the post office at any port. The commander of the vessel received one anna for each letter delivered or received.

We find the origin of the Dead Letter Office in Sections 25 to 27 of the Act. Unclaimed letters after lying for three months at any post office were to be sent to the General Post Office of the Presidency, and at intervals, not exceeding three months, lists of such unclaimed letters and packets were to be published in the Official Gazette. When letters and packets lay unclaimed for a period of eighteen months at the General Post Office, the Postmaster-General was authorized to open them and pay any valuable property found therein into the Government Treasury for the benefit of the party having a right to it. After a further period of twelve months unclaimed letters were to be destroyed.

The Governor-General in Council had the power to grant to any person the privilege of sending and receiving all letters and packets by letter post free of postage, and of sending and receiving letters and packets by bhangy on the public service free of postage. This privilege was granted to the following persons :—

His Majesty's Principal Secretaries of State.
The President and Secretaries of the Board of Control.
The Chairman, Deputy Chairman and Directors of the East India Company.
The Secretary, Deputy Secretary and Assistant Secretary at the East India House.
The Governor-General.
The Governors of Bengal, Madras and Bombay.
The Governor of Ceylon.
The Lieutenant-Governor of the North-West Provinces.
The Chief Justices of Bengal, Madras and Bombay.
The Bishops of Calcutta, Madras and Bombay.
The Members of the Supreme Council.
The Members of Council of Madras and Bombay.
The Puisne Judges of the Supreme Courts of Bengal, Madras and Bombay.
The Recorder of Prince of Wales' Island, Singapore and Malacca.

The Commander-in-Chief of His Majesty's Naval Forces.

The Commander-in-Chief of the Army in India.

The Commander-in-Chief of the Army at Madras and Bombay.

Postage was charged for letters according to the following schedules :—

Distance in miles.	*Postage for a letter not exceeding 1 tola.*
20	1 anna.
50	2 annas.
100	3 "
150	4 "
200	5 "
250	6 "
300	7 "
400	8 "
500	9 "
600	10 "
700	11 "
800	12 "
900	13 "
1000	14 "
1200	15 "
1400	1 rupee.

Single postage to be added for each additional tola or part thereof.

Special rates for distance were also fixed for :

(1) Law papers, Accounts and Vouchers attested as such, with the full signature of the sender.

(2) Newspapers, Pamphlets and other printed or engrossed papers, packed in short covers open at each end, imported matter being charged at a cheaper rate than matter printed in India.

Parcels were limited to 600 tolas (15 lbs.) in weight, and the rate was 6 annas for 50 tolas (20 oz.) for 50 miles, then 3 annas for every additional 50 tolas or part thereof for every 50 miles up to 300 miles, after which 3 annas was charged for each 50 tolas for every additional 100 miles up to 1000 miles. For 1200 miles the rate was Rs.2 as.13 for every 50 tolas, and for 1400 miles and upwards Rs.3.

By Act XX of 1838 the weight of letters and packets which could be carried by a road on which there was no bhangy post was raised from 12 to 30 tolas, and the postmaster was allowed to use his discretion in forwarding packets exceeding 30 tolas. It was also enacted that " all fines incurred under Post Office Acts shall be demanded by notice from Postmasters-General or from any Postmaster, and if not paid shall be levied together with costs on goods and chattels. If no goods are forthcoming the offender may be committed to prison for twenty-two calendar months unless the fines, etc., are sooner paid." Postmasters were authorized to detain any letter in respect of which any party was liable to a fine.

Act XVII of 1839 empowered the Governor-General in Council to alter postage duties as fixed by Sections 6 and 14 of the Act, but not to increase them.

The fact that postage rates were fixed with respect to distances in 1837 is not a matter for surprise when the state of Indian roads at the time is considered. In 1833, Shore, in his *Notes on Indian Affairs*, describes the main road between Calcutta and Benares as no better than a cart-track, and says that the only road worthy of the name in India is that between Calcutta and Barrackpore. Nor was it until 1854, with the abolition of the old

Military Boards and the establishment of the Public Works Department, that the art of road-making began to improve. It will thus be understood that in 1837 the maintenance of postal lines was a real difficulty. All mail matter had to be conveyed by runners, and a slight extra weight entailed a considerable extra cost. With the introduction of railways in 1852 and good metalled roads, upon which light wheeled carriages could be used for the conveyance of mails and passengers over long distances, a complete change in postal administration was effected, and it was no longer necessary to vary the rates for letters according to distance.

With all the advance made in postal legislation and the regulation of rates there was not yet any Controlling Head. The Post Office was managed by Postmasters-General who were also postmasters in the Presidency Towns, while Collectors of Districts had charge of post offices up-country. Receipts were still granted for every article received for despatch, and in the Bombay Presidency the addresses of all articles were entered in lists known as puttees; these were given to the postmen who brought back the addressees' signatures on them. The addresses upon all articles passing in transit through the Post Office were also recorded; bags were not used, only packets of paper or cloth.

The English Mail at this time was received once a month and, since not more than 200 lbs. weight of mails could be conveyed along the Bombay-Calcutta line in one day, a week was often required for its disposal. Originally the opium merchants had their own lines, and on these being stopped they used to send private expresses by the Government dawk, which was a great source of revenue to the Post Office.

Act XVII of 1854 marks the commencement of the organization of the Indian Post Office upon its present footing. According to its provisions the whole department was placed under the control of a Director-General; the office of Postmaster-General was separated from that of Presidency Postmaster; Postmasters-General were appointed for the direct administration and supervision of the postal services in the larger provinces and Deputy Postmasters-General, at first designated Chief Inspectors, were appointed to the less important provinces and the principal Political Agencies. Postage stamps were first introduced in 1854 and rates were fixed for the conveyance of letters irrespective of distance.[1]

In this Act the postal monopoly of the East India Company was again laid down, and the three exceptions to that monopoly were legalized, namely (1) letters sent by a private friend to be delivered on his way or journey to a person, without any hire or reward for such service; (2) letters solely concerning the affairs of the sender or receiver thereof sent by a messenger on purpose; (3) letters solely concerning goods or other property sent by land or sea, to be delivered with such goods or property without any hire or reward for carrying the same.

It was important to include these exceptions in the Act, as under the Post Office Act of 1837 there was nothing to prevent a man who sent a letter to his friend by messenger incurring a penalty of Rs.50, a fine to which both the messenger and recipient were equally liable.

[1] The first issue of postage stamps in India was actually made in 1852 by Sir Bartle Frere, Commissioner of Scinde. They were local stamps for use in Scinde only, and bore the inscription "Scinde District Dak."

The great advance made in 1854 was the introduction of postage stamps and the fixing of postage rates for letters irrespective of distance.

The rates were as follows :—

On every letter not exceeding ¼ tola in weight, 6 pies.

On every letter exceeding ¼ tola and not exceeding ½ tola in weight, 1 anna.

On every letter exceeding ½ tola and not exceeding 1 tola, 2 annas.

On every letter exceeding 1 tola and not exceeding 1½ tolas in weight, 3 annas.

On every letter exceeding 1½ tolas and not exceeding 2 tolas in weight, 4 annas.

And for every tola in weight above 2 tolas, 2 additional annas.

With respect to newspapers and engraved papers a distinction, similar to that laid down in the Act of 1837, was made between imported and locally produced matter. The former was charged with 2 annas for every 6 tolas or part thereof ; the latter was charged at the following rates :—

Two annas for a weight not exceeding 3½ tolas.

Four annas for a weight not exceeding 6 tolas, and 2 annas for every additional 3 tolas above 6 tolas.

This difference in postage encouraged the circulation of newspapers and printed matter imported from England, but the high internal rates must have greatly hampered the postal circulation of journals printed in India.

Reduced rates, but still varying with distance, were laid down for Bhangy Post according to the following scale :—

For Distances.	If not Exceeding in Weight.						
	20 tolas.	100 tolas.	200 tolas.	300 tolas.	400 tolas.	500 tolas.	600 tolas.
Miles.	Rs. a.	Rs. a.	Rs. a.	Rs. a.	Rs. a.	Rs. a.	Rs. a.
Not exceeding 100	0 2	0 4	0 8	0 12	1 0	1 4	1 8
Not exceeding 300	0 6	0 12	1 8	2 4	3 0	3 12	4 8
Not exceeding 600	0 12	1 8	3 0	4 8	6 0	7 8	9 0
Not exceeding 900	1 2	2 4	4 8	6 12	9 0	11 4	13 8
Not exceeding 1200	1 8	3 0	6 0	9 0	12 0	15 0	18 0
Exceeding 1200	1 14	3 12	7 8	11 4	15 0	18 12	22 8

Books, pamphlets, packets of newspapers and of printed and engraved papers were charged at the following rates by bhangy post :—

Not exceeding 20 tolas . . . 1 anna
Exceeding 20 tolas and not exceeding
40 tolas . . . . . 2 annas
For every 20 tolas above 40 tolas . 1 anna
provided that the total weight must
not exceed 120 tolas.

The postage on bhangy parcels was calculated by the most elaborate Polymetrical Tables which were supplied to all post offices in English and Vernacular. Many a grievous complaint was laid by members of the public against the strange methods employed by the Post Office in calculating the distance between two places. The sender of a parcel naturally considered that he should pay for the shortest distance between the place of despatch and the place of receipt, but not so the Post

Office. It decided that the "postal route," however circuitous, was the one by which postage should be calculated.

Letters were ordinarily limited to 12 tolas in weight, but by Act XX of 1838 the weight had been raised to 30 tolas upon lines where no bhangy post existed; this limit was now raised to 40 tolas (1 lb.) and, where both a bhangy and letter post were conveyed in the same carriage, a special prohibition was made that letters or packets of newspapers of less than 12 tolas weight must not be sent by bhangy post under penalty of a fine of Rs.50 for each offence. This clause was evidently introduced on account of the charge made by the railway companies for the carriage of bhangy parcels.

The 600 tola limit for parcels was continued except in special cases which were laid down by the Governor-General in Council, but in no circumstances was the weight of any parcel to exceed 2000 tolas (50 lbs.). Ship postage was levied on parcels, when conveyed by the East India Company's post by sea, at the rate of 8 annas for each 100 tolas. When any parcel had to be conveyed by bhangy as well as by sea, this postage was levied in addition to bhangy postage. Letters and newspapers for Ceylon or any place where no postal communication was established by the East India Company were dealt with as unclaimed, unless the full postage was prepaid by means of postage stamps.

With the introduction of postage stamps we now find the first regulations for encouraging the prepayment of postal articles. In Section 20 it is laid down that, where the East India Company have a postal communication, double postage shall be charged on unstamped letters at the time of delivery, and in the case of insufficiently stamped letters double the deficiency. This rule did not apply to newspapers or other printed matter, but in order to compel the public to use the new postage stamps, post offices were forbidden to accept money in prepayment of any postal articles except parcels. Redirected letters were charged with postage at prepaid rates, and a penalty of Rs.200 was imposed for sending " any explosive or other dangerous material or substance by post."

Rules were drawn up for the use and sale of postage stamps, vendors were appointed, and heavy penalties were exacted from vendors who failed to comply with the regulations. Registration of any article was allowed upon payment of a fee of 4 annas which entitled the sender to a receipt, but, strange to say, the registration fee had to be paid in cash, stamps not being recognized in payment.

The clauses of Act XVII of 1837 regarding the obligations of commanders of vessels were renewed, and also the clauses dealing with unclaimed and refused articles. The privilege of free postage was entirely abolished, but the letters and packets sent on the public service by certain officials were still carried under frank. The postage due on such articles was charged to the several public departments concerned. This measure led to wanton extravagance in the matter of official postage, no care was taken to economize either in the number or the size of " public service " articles and various abuses of franking occurred. The list of officers authorized to frank became so large that the Post Office could not exercise any proper check, and the difficulty of accounting in connection with the postage due was enormous. The first restriction was placed on franking in 1866 when the use of service stamps was made compulsory on all letters passing outside the Presidency towns or limits of the district in which they were posted, and in 1873 all franking privileges were abolished.

In Section 48 of the Act the duty of the Post Office to abide by the Customs regulations is insisted upon. Officers in charge of post offices were bound to detain articles suspected of containing anything contraband, and they could refuse to forward any parcel or packet addressed to a foreign post, unless it was accompanied by a Customs' House Pass. A long list of penalties, most of which exist at the present day, was drawn up for offences and misdemeanours committed by postal officials. Informers were encouraged by being allowed to receive half of every fine imposed, but no proceedings could be taken against any one under this Act without an order in writing from Government, the Director-General or a Postmaster-General.

In 1854 Mr. Riddell was appointed the first Director-General of the Post Office, and he compiled the first Manual of Rules to be observed by the whole Department. At this time there were 201 head-quarter offices and 451 minor offices in India, but every office kept its own accounts separately and submitted them direct to the Audit Office which was part of the Accountant General's Office. It was not until 1861 that postal accounts were removed from the Civil auditors and handed over to an officer known as the "Compiler of Post Office Accounts" and not until 1866–7 that the distinction between Head and Branch offices was made for account purposes.

The Manual of 1854 made no proper arrangement for sorting offices, it only provided for mails being received *en masse* and for their distribution afterwards to peons and into the "thana" and forwarding boxes. Every post office upon a line had to make up a separate mail packet for every office in advance, and it received one from every office in rear, a most cumbersome proceeding, which was put a stop to in 1860, when long detentions were made at certain large stations upon the main routes for the purpose of sorting the mails. Paid letters were impressed with a red date-stamp to distinguish them from unpaid, which bore a black date-stamp. Letters for foreign countries were sent with steamer postage invoices (chalans) to the different Presidency towns. Prepayment of articles sent to England via Marseilles, for which Brindisi was substituted in 1870, was not possible, nor could letters for countries like the United States be prepaid.

It seems hardly credible that in 1854 one of the longest chapters of the Manual was devoted to an elaborate system of fining, under which different offices claimed fines from one another for bad work brought to light by them. The official who detected the finable offence was allowed to keep the amount of the fine subject to a deduction of 10 per cent, which was remitted to the Postmaster-General's office to cover the cost of printing Fine Statements, Bills, etc. A regular schedule of offences with the fine allotted for each was drawn up; for instance, the missending of a mail bag was assessed at Rs.3, while the missending of a parcel or packet cost 8 annas. Naturally there was great energy expended in detecting offences for which fines were imposed, and the result was an enormous amount of correspondence and bitter recrimination between offices. This vicious practice continued for many years and was not finally put a stop to until 1880.

CHAPTER IV

LATER POSTAL REGULATIONS

By Act XIV of 1866 postage rates were still further reduced as follows :—

For letters not exceeding $\frac{1}{4}$ tola	6 pies.
Exceeding $\frac{1}{4}$ tola and not exceeding $\frac{1}{2}$ tola	1 anna.
For every additional $\frac{1}{2}$ tola . .	1 "
For newspapers not exceeding 10 tolas .	1 "
For every additional 10 tolas . .	1 "

It will be noticed that the distinction in rates between imported and local newspapers was withdrawn.

Books, pamphlets, packets, etc.—

Not exceeding 10 tolas in weight .	1 anna.
For every additional 10 tolas . .	1 "

Parcels were still charged according to the distance they had to be conveyed, but the rates were reduced. The following table gives the scale of charges :—

Distance in Miles.		Not Exceeding Tolas.															
		20 tolas.		50 tolas.		100 tolas.		200 tolas.		300 tolas.		400 tolas.		500 tolas.		600 tolas.	
		Rs.	a.	Rs.	a.	Rs.	a.	Rs.	a.	Rs.	a.	Rs.	a.	Rs.	a.	Rs.	a.
Not exceeding	300	0	4	0	8	0	12	1	8	2	4	3	0	3	12	4	8
Not exceeding	600	0	8	1	0	1	8	3	0	4	8	6	0	7	8	9	0
Not exceeding	900	0	12	1	8	2	4	4	8	6	12	9	0	11	4	13	8
Not exceeding	1200	1	0	2	0	3	0	6	0	9	0	12	0	15	0	18	0
Exceeding	1200	1	4	2	8	3	12	7	8	11	4	15	0	18	12	22	8

It was now ordered that registration upon letters, the fee for which was still fixed at 4 annas, should be prepaid in postage stamps. The penal clauses relating to counterfeiting stamps had been included in the Indian Penal Code, Act XLV of 1860, and were therefore omitted from this Act. The other penal clauses were practically the same as those that existed in the Act of 1854, and the principle is again laid down of the non-responsibility of Government for any loss or damage which may occur in respect of anything entrusted to the Post Office for conveyance.

From 1866 the work of the Post Office began to develop enormously, and its functions had to be gradually extended to meet the growing needs of the public. In 1869 the charge on redirected letters was abolished and the letter postage rates were further reduced as follows:—

For letters not exceeding ½ tola . .	6 pies.
Exceeding ½ tola but not exceeding 1 tola	1 anna.
For every additional tola or fraction thereof	1 "

The antiquated system of making parcel post rates vary with distance could no longer be maintained, and in 1871 a system of rates which varied with weight, irrespective of distance, was introduced. A parcel post service was established between India and England in 1873, but the collection and distribution of parcels were at first effected through the agency of the Peninsular and Oriental Steamship Company, and it was not until 1885 that the Post Offices of both countries undertook the management of the parcel post. In 1873 special postage rates were introduced for official articles, namely:

Not exceeding ½ tola	½ anna.
Not exceeding 10 tolas	1 "
Not exceeding 20 tolas	5 annas.
Not exceeding 30 tolas	10 "
Every additional 10 tolas	5 "

At the same time it was laid down that official covers from Government offices should be prepaid by means of service postage stamps.

Under the provision of the Act of Parliament (III–IV Vict. Cap. 69) soldiers and seamen were allowed the privilege of sending letters not exceeding half an ounce in weight at the rate of 1d. for each letter. This rate was introduced into India in 1854, and 8 pies was reckoned the equivalent of 1d. In 1874 the postage on such letters was fixed at 9 pies for half an ounce owing to the increase in the rate of exchange. In 1899 the Imperial Penny Postage scheme was introduced, by which the initial rate of postage to the United Kingdom and to certain British colonies and possessions was fixed at 1 anna for a letter not exceeding half an ounce in weight, so that the privilege enjoyed by soldiers and seamen was no longer of any advantage, and when in 1907 the initial rate under the Imperial Penny Postage Scheme was raised from half an ounce to 1 ounce there was no further object in retaining this special concession.

In 1877 the Value-Payable or Cash on Delivery system was introduced, and in 1878 the Post Office undertook the insurance of letters and parcels. At first there was no limit to the amount for which an article could be insured, until a claim for the contents of a parcel insured for Rs.60,000 showed the enormous liabilities which the Department might incur under this system. Accordingly, in 1890 the limit was fixed at Rs.1000, but was raised in 1898 to Rs.2000, and the procedure was greatly simplified. The insurance fee was originally fixed at one-half per cent, which was subsequently reduced to a quarter, and in 1905 to one-eighth per cent.

Previous to 1880 the money order work of the country was carried on by the Government Treasuries, and the procedure was rather cumbersome; in that year it was handed over to the Post Office, with the result that in a few months the number of money orders issued and paid quadrupled. The extent to which money order business has increased may be gauged from the fact that the value of inland money orders in 1880–81 was 45 millions, and in 1917–18 it had increased to over 617 millions of rupees.

In 1870 Government Savings Banks were first established in India in connection with District Treasuries, and in 1882 permission was given to open savings bank accounts at post offices, but the management and control of the funds still remained with the Treasuries. In 1885 all savings banks at Treasuries were closed and the business was transferred entirely to the Post Office. The general development of this branch will be treated of in the chapter on Savings Banks, but, as an example of the growth of business, the figures of 1882–83 and of 1913–14 are remarkable. In 1882–83 there were 39,121 depositors with a balance of Rs.27,96,730; in 1913–14 there were 1,638,725 depositors with a balance of Rs.23,16,75,467.

In 1883 combined post and telegraph offices were introduced, and it is no exaggeration to say that these are solely responsible for the extension of telegraph facilities to the smaller markets and rural tracts of India. In 1884 the sale of British postal orders was authorized, and the same year marks the introduction of Postal Life Insurance, a measure at first confined to servants of the Department but afterwards extended to all Government servants. In 1890, at the request of the military authorities, the Post Office undertook the payment of military pensioners in the Punjab.

In this way the Department has grown. From being a mere agency for the carriage of correspondence and parcels in 1866, the Post Office has now become the poor man's bank; it does an enormous value-payable and money order business; it is an important insurance agency and pension paymaster, and to such an extent have postage rates been reduced in India that it would be hard to find a man who could not afford to communicate by post with his friends.

Needless to say, the Post Office Act of 1866 was quite unsuited to modern needs, and Act VI of 1898 was framed to deal with the new requirements of postal work. The 1866 Act was amended by Act III of 1882, which authorized any officer of the Post Office empowered in this behalf by the Governor-General in Council to search for newspapers regarding which a notification had been published under the Sea Customs Act. By Act III of 1895 powers were provided in accordance with the general policy of the Postal Union for dealing with fictitious or previously used postage stamps of other countries found on articles received from abroad, and by Act XVI of 1896 the Post Office was authorized to collect Customs duty paid in advance in the same manner as postage under the Act.

Act VI of 1898 is to a great extent an Enabling Act which reserves to Government the power of dealing by rule with numerous questions of postal practice and procedure affecting the public. For the first time legal recognition was given to registered newspapers, and the Governor-General in Council was empowered to make rules for their registration in the offices of Postmasters-General. The acceptance of the official marks of the Post Office on postal articles as prima facie evidence that they have been refused, that the addressee cannot be found, or that any sum is due on them, was a principle taken from the English Law.

Section 20 of the Act was quite new and prohibits the sending by post of indecent or obscene articles, and the tendency of the age is shown by the first mention in this clause of the word " sedition " in connection with postal articles. " Articles having thereon or on the cover thereof any words, marks or designs of an indecent, obscene, seditious, defamatory or grossly offensive character " were prohibited from being sent by post. The wording of this section is interesting owing to the difficulty of interpreting the meaning of the word " thereon " ; it would almost seem that the framers of the Act wished to wrap this clause in ambiguity. In Section 22 the important principle of the English Law is laid down that the Post Office is not bound to send parcels and packets along with the letter mail, but may detain them as long as is necessary. By Section 25 special power is given to search for goods notified under the Sea Customs Act, and in Section 26, the Public Emergency section, " The Governor-General in Council, or a Local Government, or any officer specially authorized in this behalf by the Governor-General in Council, may, by an order in writing, direct that any postal article or class or description of postal articles in course of transmission by post shall be intercepted or detained." Had the framers of this Act any idea of the extent to which this power would have to be used they might have expressed themselves in greater detail.[1] Sections 30 to 36 and 43 to 48 of the Act deal with the power of the Governor-General in Council to make rules for the insurance of postal articles and the transmission of value-payable articles and money orders by post.

To judge from the large number of additional penalty clauses introduced into this Act, postal crime seems to have grown side by side with postal development. Every possible misdemeanour and fraud is visited with appropriate punishment ; not even the mail runner who fails in his duty to appear at the time he is required can escape, while the postman who makes a false entry in his book to show that he has been visiting a certain village, when all the time he has been loitering in a neighbouring bazaar, renders himself liable to six months' imprisonment or a fine of one hundred rupees. Sections 62 and 63 are taken from the English Post Office Protection Act, 1884, and impose penalties for injuring the contents of any letter-box or for disfiguring any post office or letter-box. To prevent hasty and ill-considered prosecutions, it was laid

[1] The first instance of an article being prohibited from passing through the post is that of the *Bengal Gazette* (editor, J. A. Hicky), quoted by Dr. Busteed in his *Echoes of Old Calcutta :*

"*Order.* Fort William, November 14th, 1780. Public notice is hereby given that as a weekly newspaper called the *Bengal Gazette* or *Calcutta General Advertiser*, printed by J. A. Hicky, has lately been found to contain several unbroken paragraphs tending to vilify private characters and to disturb the peace of the Settlement, it is no longer permitted to be circulated through the channel of the General Post Office."

down in Section 72 that no Court should take cognizance of any offence under the Act, except with the previous sanction or on the complaint of the Director-General of the Post Office or of a Postmaster-General.

In 1898 postage rates on letters were reduced to the following scale:—

Not exceeding ½ tola . . .	½ anna.
" " 1½ tolas . . .	1 "
" " 3 " . . .	2 annas.
For every additional 1½ tolas or fraction thereof	1 anna.

The postage on newspapers was fixed at:

Not exceeding 4 tolas . . .	¼ anna.
" " 20 " . . .	½ "
For every additional 20 tolas or part thereof	½ "

In 1905 a still further reduction in letter postage was made, namely:

Not exceeding ¾ tola . . .	½ anna.
" " 1½ tolas . . .	1 "
" " 3 " . . .	2 annas.
For every additional 1½ tolas or fraction thereof	1 anna.

In 1907, after a long discussion, it was decided to make the Indian anna rate approximate to the English penny rate. The British Post Office had decided to carry 4 ounces for one penny, and as an ounce is roughly 2½ tolas the weight that could be sent for an anna was increased from 1½ to 10 tolas. The ¾ tolas for ½ anna was very properly considered absurd, and the weight was raised to 1 tola. The rates as revised in 1907 were:

Not exceeding 1 tola	½ anna.
" " 10 tolas	1 "
For every additional 10 tolas or fraction thereof	1 anna.

This was a sweeping measure which mainly benefited that portion of the community which could best afford to pay high rates of postage, and the argument for making the anna rate correspond to the penny rate in England left out of account the very important fact that in England the minimum rate for letters was a penny, whereas in India it is half that amount. It is difficult to estimate what the loss to the Post Office must have been, but when one considers that a letter of 10 tolas, which under the previous rates would have had to bear 7 annas postage, could be sent for 1 anna it will be understood that the loss was considerable. The measure was also one that affected the Post Office in two ways, since less revenue was received in postage stamps and the increased number of bulky letters necessitated a larger carrying staff. Despite the admitted cheapness of postage in India, some short-sighted agitators cry out for a ¼ anna letter rate; but the Post Office can well afford to disregard their murmurings and may congratulate itself on having made its services accessible to even the very poorest member of the community.

By Act III of 1912 the Indian Post Office Act of 1898 was further amended, and special rules were made to protect postmasters who had to search or detain articles passing through the post. The public who use the value-payable system have been protected from fraudulent

GROUP OF SENIOR OFFICERS IN 1898

C. STEWART-WILSON G. S. CURTIS W. MAXWELL C. J. BADSHAH

J. CORNWALL H. M. KISCH SIR ARTHUR FANSHAWE *Director General* A. T. FORBES

traders by a section which provides for the retention and repayment to the addressee, in cases of fraud, of money recovered on the delivery of any value-payable postal article; at the same time the Post Office is authorized to levy a fee before making any inquiry into complaints of this kind.

Since the Great War broke out in 1914 it has been found necessary to increase inland postage rates for both letters and parcels. In 1918 the letter rates were fixed as follows:—

For letters: Not exceeding 1 tola .	½ anna.
Exceeding 1 tola, but not exceeding 2½ tolas	1 ,,
For every additional 2½ tolas or part thereof	1 ,,
For parcels: Not exceeding 20 tolas .	2 annas.
Exceeding 20 tolas, but not exceeding 40 tolas	4 ,,
For every additional 40 tolas or part thereof	4 ,,

Many complaints were received that the parcel rates were excessive and injuring the fruit trade and other local industries, so that with effect from the 1st June, 1919, the rates were reduced to 3 annas for every 40 tolas up to 440 tolas, the minimum of 2 annas for 20 tolas remaining the same.

CHAPTER V

PARCEL POST

THE parcel post in India has its origin in the old "Bhangy Post," a name derived from the bamboo stick or bhangy which an Indian carrier balances on his shoulder with the weights slung at each end. The Bhangy Post was first used solely for the conveyance of official records and articles sent on Government service, and the limit of weight was 600 tolas (15 lbs.). In 1854 a regular Bhangy Post was established and opened to the public. The rates varied with weight and distance according to the scale laid down in the Post Office Act of 1854. Where communication by rail existed, the practice was to hand over bhangy parcels to the railway at the latter's risk and to demand their conveyance to destination free of charge. This procedure led to a series of those acrimonious disputes which are so characteristic of the early relations between the Post Office and the railway companies. The contention of the Post Office was that the bhangy mail formed part of the regular mail which the railway was bound by law to carry free of charge. The East India Railway, which took up the cudgels on the other side, denied this contention and insisted upon charging for parcels as goods sent by passenger train. Finally, after much wrangling, the matter was settled by Government in 1855, when it was decided that service bhangy parcels should be carried free and that the rate for non-service parcels should be fixed at ⅓ anna per maund (80 lbs.) per mile, which was the existing rate for passengers' luggage. At the same time the Post Office was directed to withdraw from the carrier traffic wherever the railway could supply its place, and post offices were forbidden to accept non-service bhangy parcels for places situated on railway lines.

These rules were not very effective, since it was impossible to distinguish service from non-service parcels or to ascertain the weight of the latter when they were both despatched together and lump sum payments were accepted. The amounts paid show that the traffic cannot have been very great; for instance, in 1871 the Great India Peninsula Railway agreed to accept a monthly payment of Rs.568, the Madras Railway Rs.173 and the Bombay, Baroda and Central India Railway Rs.150, which was afterwards raised to Rs.400 in 1881. The whole question was soon merged in that of general haulage rates for postal vehicles, which is discussed in the chapter upon the Railway Mail Service.

The statement at the end of this chapter shows the variation in parcel rates from 1866 to 1919. The first great step forward in the administration of the parcel post was in 1871, when rates according to distance were abolished and a fixed rate of 3 annas for 10 tolas was introduced. The limits of weight were retained at 600 tolas for foot lines and 2000 tolas for railway lines, which were fixed in 1869. In 1895 rates were reduced and registration for all parcels exceeding 440 tolas in weight was made compulsory. In 1907, after a strong representation made by the Railway Conference that the parcel post was interfering with the railway parcel traffic, the limit of weight was lowered to 800 tolas (20 lbs.). As a matter of fact, after a careful inquiry it was found that very few parcels above this weight were carried by the Post Office and that these were carried at a loss. In the same year the rates for small parcels were greatly reduced, with the result that the total number carried in 1907–8 increased by over 600,000. The railways did not gain much by the concession, as the retail dealers adopted the simple device of packing their goods in smaller bulk, which the low rates enabled them to do without any appreciable loss.

The development of parcel traffic since 1854 is shown by the following figures :—

	Number of Parcels.
1854–55	463,000
1870–71	694,000
1880–81	1,080,868
1890–91	1,901,547
1900–01	2,679,119
1910–11	11,205,844
1913–14	12,667,172
1917–18	14,150,948

The increase in the last few years is little short of marvellous and is due to the reduction in rates and the growth of the value-payable or cash on delivery system so largely adopted by all retail traders, which has diverted the whole of the light parcel traffic from the railways to the Post Office.

In 1873 an overland Parcel Post was established between Great Britain and India through the agency of the Peninsular and Oriental Steam Navigation Company. The British Post Office had no concern with this arrangement, and in 1885 a direct exchange, which was quite separate from the P. & O. Company's contract, was introduced between the two administrations for parcels up to a limit of seven pounds in weight. In 1897, at the Universal Postal Congress held at Washington, India joined the International Parcel Post Union, and since 1899, when the Acts of the Congress came into force, parcels can be exchanged with almost any country in the world.

As already mentioned, nothing has affected the parcel post traffic of the country to such an extent as the value-payable or cash on delivery system, which was introduced in 1878 and is now used generally by all retail firms in India. By this system the Post Office not only undertakes to deliver a parcel, but also, for a small commission, to collect the cost of it from the addressee. In India, where there are few large firms outside the Presidency towns, the value-payable system has proved an inestimable convenience to the upcountry purchaser, who pays the Post Office for his purchases on receipt and is put to no further trouble. Like everything designed for the good of mankind, the Value-Payable Post is not altogether an unmixed blessing, and it is a source of continual worry to the officials of the Department. The weak point in the system is that people have to buy articles without seeing them, and if they are disappointed in their purchases they are inclined to think that the Post Office is at fault and to demand their money back. It is customary in India for certain ladies to dispose of their garments through the medium of the advertisement columns of the *Pioneer*, one of the leading newspapers. The dresses are always by Paquin and quite new; the hats are the latest from Paris. This is the seller's point of view. How different that of the purchaser! As Postmaster-General I have received many a bitter complaint of the rag which has been received under the name of a new Paquin gown and for which I apparently was held personally responsible. "I never imagined that the Post Office could lend its assistance to such disgraceful swindling," once wrote an indignant lady who had suffered in this way and who was told that the Department could not possibly adjudicate on the quality of the goods received by her, that the Department was only in the position of carriers and that she must settle her dispute with the sender.

The value-payable system suffers chiefly from the firm belief in Providence which is so deeply engrained in the Eastern mind. Although strictly forbidden by the rules of the Post Office, the small trader sends out numbers of articles by value-payable post to persons who have not given any orders for them, trusting that some of them will be accepted by a confiding public, and, strange to say, he manages to do a certain amount of business in this way. On the other hand, many people are quite ready to order things from shops which they hope to be able to pay for upon arrival, but, unfortunately for the firms that supply them, these hopes are often not fulfilled. The Indian schoolboy, who is very like all other schoolboys in the world in this respect, is specially tempted by the flashy catalogues issued by the cheap Calcutta firms, and when, in the enthusiasm of the moment, he orders a five rupee watch, it doesn't follow that he has the money or is even likely to have it; but his self-esteem is satisfied by the mere issue of the order and, as for his ability to pay when the time comes, it lies on the knees of the gods. The result of this trait in Eastern character is that about 20 per cent of the value-payable articles posted are returned to the senders.

Some years ago a firm of box-makers who wanted to push their business discovered that the value-payable post, assisted by the national character, provided them with a royal road to success, and they set to work on the following lines. They issued a large number of tickets by post, which were delivered on payment of 1 rupee and 2 annas. Any person who was innocent enough to accept one of these found that the ticket was composed of six coupons, and that if he could induce six of his friends to send the coupons to the firm and each to receive in return a similar ticket *and pay for it,* then he as the original recipient would be presented with a steel trunk. The success of this scheme was extraordinary, and every post office in India was flooded with these coupon tickets. About 70 per cent were refused, but the firm lost nothing by this, as it saved them in the matter of trunks, since, if any one of the coupon holders failed to keep faith with his friend the bargain was off. The whole business was a gigantic swindle, and it so offended the Director-General's sense of morality that he had a regulation passed to put a stop to any articles being sent by post which contained " coupons, tickets, certificates or introductions for the sale of goods on what is known as the snowball system."

A complete history of the Indian Parcel Post would require the pen of a military historian. It is a history of warfare with continuous engagements, sometimes regular pitched battles with the railways and sometimes small but sharp skirmishes with irate ladies. The latest foes are the municipal councils of certain large towns in which the revenue is raised by an octroi tax upon all imported articles. Hitherto articles received by post have been exempt from any tax of this kind, and all attempts made by municipalities to be allowed to scrutinize the parcel post have been strenuously opposed. The thin end of the wedge has, however, been introduced at Delhi, where lists of insured parcels are supplied to the municipality, which makes its own arrangements for ascertaining the contents from the addressees. The practice is wrong in principle, because it is a breach of the confidence which the public place in the Post Office on the understanding that no information of any kind regarding postal articles is imparted except to the persons immediately concerned, and any measure which tends to shake the confidence of the public in the secrecy of the Department is to be strongly deprecated. A great deal of fuss was made in Simla some years ago about this very matter on the ground that the local traders suffered from people purchasing goods outside the municipality and getting them in by post. When an inquiry was held, it was found that the large majority of parcels received by post were addressed to the firms in the town, a discovery which put a sudden stop to the agitation. It is very doubtful if the Parcel Post at the present rates pays the Post Office, and where places are situated some distance off the line of rail and have to be reached by foot lines it is quite certain that every parcel is carried at a loss. Unfortunately these are the very places where people make the greatest use of the Parcel Post; the tea planters of Assam, for example, getting their whisky, jam and other stores in this way from Calcutta.

A further agitation is now afoot to have the weight of parcels brought down to eleven pounds, which is the maximum weight for a foreign parcel and is also the limit of weight in England. This, on the whole, is as much as the Post Office can be fairly expected to carry, but whether the proposal will be adopted remains to be seen.

Parcel Post Rates

(1) Rates of postage on inland parcels in force from 1866 to 31st March, 1878 :

For Distances		If not Exceeding in Weight															
		20 tolas.		50 tolas.		100 tolas.		200 tolas.		300 tolas.		400 tolas.		500 tolas.		600 tolas.	
	Miles	Rs.	a.	Rs.	a.	Rs.	a.	Rs.	a.	Rs.	a.	Rs.	a.	Rs.	a.	Rs.	a.
Not exceeding	300	0	4	0	8	0	12	1	8	2	4	3	0	3	12	4	8
Not exceeding	600	0	8	1	0	1	8	3	0	4	8	6	0	7	8	9	0
Not exceeding	900	0	12	1	8	2	4	4	8	6	12	9	0	11	3	41	8
Not exceeding	1200	1	0	2	0	3	0	6	0	9	0	12	0	15	0	18	0
Exceeding	1200	1	4	2	8	3	12	7	8	11	4	15	0	18	12	22	8

(2) Rates of postage on inland parcels in force from 1st April, 1878, to 14th August, 1880 :

Not exceeding 40 tolas in weight .	8 annas.
Exceeding 40 tolas and not exceeding 80 tolas	12 „
For every additional 40 tolas . .	4 „

(3) Rates of postage on inland parcels in force from 15th August, 1880, to 31st July, 1895 :

Not exceeding 20 tolas in weight .	4 annas.
Exceeding 20 tolas and not exceeding 40 tolas	8 „
For every additional 40 tolas . .	4 „

(4) Rates of postage on inland parcels in force from 1st August, 1895, to 30th June, 1901 :

Any parcel not exceeding 20 tolas in weight	2 annas.

Any parcel exceeding 20 tolas, but not exceeding 40 tolas in weight . 4 annas.

For each additional 40 tolas or fraction of 40 tolas up to 2000 tolas . 4 „

Registration fee (optional for uninsured parcels not exceeding 440 tolas in weight)—

For a parcel not exceeding 20 tolas in weight . . . . . . 2 annas.

For a parcel exceeding 20 tolas in weight . . . . . . 4 „

(5) Rates of postage on inland parcels in force from 1st July, 1901, to 30th September, 1907:

(*a*) Parcels not exceeding 440 tolas in weight—

For a parcel not exceeding 20 tolas in weight . . . . . . 2 annas.

For a parcel exceeding 20 tolas, but not exceeding 40 tolas in weight 4 „

For every additional 40 tolas or part of that weight . . . . 2 „

(*b*) Parcels exceeding 440 tolas in weight—

For a parcel exceeding 440 tolas, but not exceeding 480 tolas in weight Rs.3

For every additional 40 tolas or part of that weight . . . . 4 annas.

(6) Rates of postage on inland parcels in force from 1st October, 1907, to 31st October, 1918:

(*a*) Parcels not exceeding 440 tolas in weight—

For a parcel not exceeding 40 tolas in weight . . . . . . 2 annas.

For every additional 40 tolas or part of that weight . . . . 2 „

SIR WILLIAM MAXWELL, K.C.I.E.
DIRECTOR GENERAL POSTS AND TELEGRAPHS 1913—1918

(*b*) Parcels exceeding 440 tolas in weight—

For a parcel exceeding 440 tolas, but not exceeding 480 tolas . .	Rs.3
For every additional 40 tolas or part of that weight	4 annas.

(7) From 1st October, 1908, the maximum limit of weight for an inland parcel was reduced from 2000 tolas to 800 tolas in the case of a private (non-official) parcel, and raised from 600 tolas to 800 tolas in the case of an official parcel.

(8) Rates of postage on inland parcels in force from 1st November, 1918, to 15th May, 1919:

For a parcel not exceeding 20 tolas .	2 annas.
For a parcel exceeding 20 tolas, but not exceeding 40 tolas . . .	4 "
For every additional 40 tolas or part of that weight up to 800 tolas .	4 "

(9) Rates of postage on inland parcels in force from 16th May, 1919, up to date:

(*a*) Parcels not exceeding 440 tolas in weight—

For a parcel not exceeding 20 tolas .	2 annas.
For a parcel exceeding 20 tolas, but not exceeding 40 tolas . . .	3 "
For every additional 40 tolas or part of that weight	3 "

(*b*) Parcels exceeding 440 tolas in weight—

For a parcel exceeding 440 tolas, but not exceeding 480 tolas . .	Rs.3
For every additional 40 tolas or part of that weight	4 annas,

CHAPTER VI

THE RAILWAY MAIL SERVICE

ONE of the most important branches of the Post Office is the Railway Mail Service, which used to be called the Travelling Post Office. The railways are the arteries through which the very life-blood of the Department flows, and it is upon the arrangements for the conveyance of mails by rail that proper postal administration depends. Before 1863 the mail bags were carried in the guard's van if the weight was small, but when the mail was heavy a separate compartment in charge of a mail guard was used. As there was no intermediate sorting, every post office had to make up a packet or bag for every other post office in front, and these various packets were received and delivered at each station by the mail guard. In a short time the number of such packets became quite unmanageable, and the inconvenience and delay in disposing of them considerable, so that, in order to make it possible to sort the mails between North-West India and Calcutta, long detentions had to be made at Allahabad, Cawnpore and Benares, otherwise letters could not possibly be sent direct to their destinations. In 1860 a solution of the difficulty was proposed by Mr. Riddell, Director-General of the Post Office, namely, the establishment of a Travelling Post Office between Calcutta and Raneegunge, but the Government of

India refused to sanction it. In 1863, however, a sorting section was established on the Great Indian Peninsula Railway between Allahabad and Cawnpore, but no regular service was organized until 1870, when the frontier Travelling Post Office was introduced under a Superintendent with his head-quarters at Allahabad. In 1877 the designation of this Officer was altered to Chief Superintendent, T.P.O., and in 1880 to Inspector-General, Railway Mail Service. The Inspector-General worked as an Assistant Director-General in the Direction until 1890, but in that year he was placed in a much more independent position as an administrative officer. Owing to the large increase in the mileage of the Railway Mail Service it was found impossible for one man to exercise an efficient control over it, and in 1905 a Deputy Inspector-General was appointed; but even with his assistance the work was too heavy, and in 1907 the whole of India was divided into four circles and each of them placed under the jurisdiction of an officer designated Inspector-General, Railway Mail Service and Sorting, known by the wits of the Department as an Inspector-General of sorts. The gentlemen with this sesquipedalian title control the railways or portions of railways in their own circles. In 1918 their number was reduced to three by the abolition of the Southern Circle, and their designation was altered to Deputy Postmaster-General, Railway Mail Service.

The main conditions under which a railway should carry mails were laid down in Clause 20 of the contract made with the East Indian Railway in 1849, and was as follows: "That the said Railway Company will at all times during the said determinable term convey on the said Railway the Government mails and post bags and the guards and other servants of the Post Office in charge thereof free of charge." A similar condition existed in the contract with the Great Indian Peninsula Railway, but the Companies contended that the conveyance of mails did not include the haulage of sorting carriages in which sorters were employed. The Post Office refused to accept this view and nasty things were said on both sides. The Post Office seemed to think that railways had been invented for the conveyance of mails without any regard to dividends, while the railways regarded the Post Office as a confounded nuisance and its officials as unscrupulous thieves. It was finally settled that two compartments of a second-class carriage should be set apart and specially fitted for the Travelling Post Office on ordinary mail trains free of charge. If a special carriage was required in addition, then the haulage rate of 1½ annas a mile would be charged, and the rate for special trains was fixed at Rs.3–8 a mile. With respect to the cost and maintenance of postal vehicles it was decided that, if they were paid for by Government in the first instance, the charge for maintenance only should be incurred, but, if the Companies had to bear the cost of construction, then the charge should include the cost of maintenance, the interest on capital and the cost of restoring the vehicles when worn out.

The settlement between the Post Office and the Railways did not last long. Despite their acquiescence in the regulations which had been laid down, the Companies refused to abide by them and repeated demands were made for the cost of hauling postal vans. On the Great Indian Peninsula Railway everything possible was done to hamper the work of the Department, parcel bags were deliberately left behind at stations, postal vans were cut off at way-side places without any warning and there never was any certainty that the whole mail would reach its destination. In 1879 the nuisance became so intolerable that petitions were made by the public for the interference of Government, and after some deliberation a settlement was made with this Railway on the following terms :—

(1) The Post Office was to pay Rs.6000 a month for the ordinary services performed for it by the Railway, and for this payment a large fitted van with a well and extra vans for weekly foreign mails would be supplied.

(2) The price for additional reserved accommodation was raised from 18 to 30 pies a mile on each vehicle.

In 1882 the Government of India prescribed definite sizes for postal vans and called them standard full and standard half vans, and arrangements were made with the East Indian and Madras Railways to accept 8 annas a mile as the haulage of a standard van. Various agreements were made with the other railways, some of which claimed payment not for haulage but for the conveyance of bhangy parcels, and in some cases lump sum payments were made annually to cover all services. For instance, the Darjeeling Steam Tramway was given a fixed sum of Rs.10,260 annually, which represented exactly the cost of the old tonga line between Siliguri and Darjeeling.

The question of haulage of postal vans and of payment for the carriage of mails was finally settled in connection with State Railways. In 1877 it was ruled by the

Governor-General in Council that the conveyance of mails over State Railways should be paid for. The question was raised with reference to the conveyance of mails on the Hathras-Muttra (Provincial) Railway, and it was decided that the actual cost of carrying the mails on all Imperial and Provincial railways should be borne by the Post Office. The rules regarding payment on all State lines, both broad and metre gauge, were:

(1) Eighteen pies per vehicle per mile to be levied in proportion to the space occupied by the Postal Department.

(2) For mail bags and parcels sent in luggage vans in charge of railway guards, the amount to be paid was fixed at 1½ pies per maund (80 lbs.) per mile.

(3) Accounts to be settled half-yearly and the space as well as weight charged to be adjusted for the six months on the basis of actual space allotted (as above) and actual weight carried on the 1st June and the 1st December of each year.

(4) All officers and servants of the Postal Department travelling in the mail compartment to be carried without passes. All officials of the Travelling Post Office not travelling in the mail compartment to be carried free on being furnished with passes under the revised free pass rules. All other officers of the Postal Department to pay usual fares.

(5) A list to be kept of all free passes issued.

(6) These arrangements to have effect from the 1st April, 1877, and to remain in force until the 1st April, 1884. All claims against the Postal

Department to be settled in accordance therewith without delay, and adjusted in the accounts of the current official year. No arrear adjustment to be made in respect of any claims other than those arising out of the vehicle charge at 18 pies a mile.

Some misunderstanding seems to have arisen on the State Railways regarding the half-yearly calculations mentioned in paragraph 3, and the question of ferry charges upon Railway steamers was also raised. There was also a certain amount of disagreement about the construction and maintenance of Post Office vehicles, and on the 23rd May, 1884, Government issued a Resolution to the following effect :—

(1) That from the 1st April, 1884, and until further orders the following rules shall determine the payment for the haulage of Post Office vehicles, etc., on State Railways, and for the conveyance of mails by State Railway ferry steamers, and that they shall be applied to the East Indian Railway under the terms of Clause 18 of the Company's contract.

(2) With reference to the ruling laid down by the Government of India Public Works Department Circular No. 7R, dated the 3rd April, 1877, that the actual expenses incurred for the carriage of mails on all Imperial and Provincial Railways shall be paid by the Postal Department, the charges on all State lines, both broad and metre gauge, for the carriage of mails shall be based on a fixed rate of 18 pies per vehicle per mile, and shall be levied in proportion to the

space actually allotted to the Postal Department on its own requisition.

(3) For mail bags and parcels sent in luggage vans in charge of Railway guards the amount to be paid by the Postal Department shall be 1 pie per maund per mile. Under this rule mails may be despatched either

(*a*) as a regular daily service according to lists supplied to the Traffic Managers for each half-year ; or

(*b*) as occasional despatches not provided for in the list, a voucher being given for each despatch ; occasional despatches should be restricted to a weight of 5 maunds for each despatch.

(4) In addition to the above, a charge equal to $4\frac{1}{2}$ per cent per annum on the original cost shall be paid by the Postal Department for all vans or parts of carriages, built or altered on its own requisition since the 1st January, 1878, for the exclusive use of the Post Office.

(5) In the event of the mileage run on the requisition of the Post Office officials by any special postal vans and compartments specially fitted for Post Office work (so as to be unuseable with convenience for ordinary traffic) being in any half-year greater in one direction than in the other, the charge for haulage shall be made, not on actual distance run, but on double the highest run in one direction. For this purpose the Railway Administration will keep a register of the up and down daily mileage of all special postal vans or compartments as aforesaid, but

this mileage is not to be used as the basis of a charge against the Postal Department in supersession of the procedure laid down in paragraph 8 below unless there is a considerable difference between the requisitioned up and down mileages.

(6) With respect to the conveyance of mails by State Railway ferry steamers where the distance traversed is 10 miles and less, an addition on account of the ferry should be made to the bill for railway service, calculated at the same mileage rate as the railway charge laid down in paragraph 2, but the addition shall not be less than 8 annas for each trip across the river.

(7) When the ferry service is over 10 miles and reserved sorting accommodation is not required or provided on board, the charge shall be separately calculated at the rate of 1 pie per maund per mile. If reserved accommodation is required, the rate of charge will be the same as for a whole carriage, viz. 18 pies per mile.

(8) Accounts are to be settled half-yearly, and the space as well as weight to be paid for shall be adjusted for the six months on the basis of actual space allotted (paragraph 2) and actual weight carried (paragraphs 3(*a*) and 7) on the 1st June and the 1st December of each year, or on such other date as may be mutually agreed upon. It is to be assumed that the actual service, inclusive of mileage, rendered on these dates is constant throughout the six months. Payments under paragraph 3(*b*) will be made monthly on bills supported by vouchers.

Regarding interest on capital outlay (paragraph 4) and the mileage of special postal vans (paragraph 5), the accounts should be rendered for the half-year ending the 31st May and the 30th November. The bills for the services rendered to the Postal Department by State Railways should be made out as above, submitted for acceptance in the months of January and July and adjusted in the accounts for February and August in each year, excepting bills for occasional despatches (paragraph 3*b*) which will be adjusted in the month after presentation of the bills.

(9) All officers and servants of the Postal Department travelling in the Post Office vans or compartments shall be carried without passes. All officers of the Railway Mail Service and the officers and employés named in Government of India letter No. 2604R of 16th January, 1879, not so travelling will be carried free on being furnished with passes under the State Railways Free Pass Rules. All other officers of the Postal Department will pay the ordinary fares.

(10) A list shall be kept of all free passes issued and periodically recorded in the minutes of official meetings.

All the larger railways in their renewed contracts with Government have agreed to accept these State Railways Rules for the conveyance of mails.

In 1886 the Government of India Public Works Department issued the following addenda to the above :

(1) In addition to the above the Postal Department shall hereafter pay, in the first instance, the

original cost of building or fitting up all vans or parts of carriages required for its use as well as the cost, when no longer required by the Post Office, of reconverting them for railway purposes.

(2) The Postal Department shall also pay interest at 4½ per cent on the original cost of all vehicles now in use, built or altered on its own requisition since the 1st January, 1878, for the exclusive use of the Post Office until such time as it may desire to repay the aforesaid original cost.

These are the rules that still govern the dealings between the Post Office and railways, and at the risk of being wearisome I have quoted them *in extenso*. In 1910 the Railway Conference Association started an agitation that the haulage rates paid were insufficient, and that by comparison with those paid for goods they were performing the work of the Post Office at a considerable loss. The result of an inquiry into their demands for an increase was an offer from the Director-General to increase the rate on broad-gauge lines to 24 pies a mile and to retain the existing rate of 18 pies on narrow-gauge lines. This offer was accepted provisionally by the Railway Conference Association in 1913, but the narrow-gauge railways were not very enthusiastic about an arrangement which put four hundred thousand rupees annually into the pockets of their colleagues and gave them nothing but the honour and glory of having deprived the Post Office of a portion of its earnings.

Until the last few years the Railway Mail Service was by far the most unpopular branch under the administration of the Post Office. The pay was bad, the hours of duty were long, the work was trying and the discomfort of the old postal vans baffled description. In the hot weather they were like ovens and, being closed in with sorting cases, it was difficult to get a through current of air. The lighting, provided by indifferent oil lamps, was injurious to the sight and did not lend itself to accurate sorting. The sorters started life on Rs.15 a month; they could not ordinarily hope for more than Rs.60 at the end of thirty years' service, and the result was an inefficient and discontented body of men with not a small proportion of rogues. Since the beginning of the present century the immense importance of the Railway Mail Service to the proper working of the Department has been recognized. Salaries have been greatly increased, and the best sorters are picked for appointments as inspectors and Assistant Superintendents. The vans have been improved, and the bogies in which the large sections work are comparatively comfortable. They are fitted with electric light and fans, and work is carried on in them under the most favourable conditions. In the old days a continuous duty of twelve hours in the train was an ordinary occurrence, and it is not a matter for surprise that men, exhausted by hard work and travel in a temperature of 110 degrees, made absurd mistakes. The length of the beats has now been reduced, rest houses have been provided at the out-stations and every man gets a sufficient time off duty upon his return to head-quarters. The new conditions have attracted men of much higher qualifications and position, and it has now been found possible to entrust the R.M.S. with almost the whole sorting of the Post Office. In important offices sorting for the outward mail is usually performed in a mail office at the railway station, the great advantage being that skilled men are employed and that, by concentrating the work in one place, economy both in staff and bags is effected. For instance, if the Calcutta G.P.O. and its sixty-three town sub-offices each perform their own sorting they must each make up separate bags or bundles for a large number of important towns and R.M.S. sections with which they are in postal communication; but if they despatch their mail to a central sorting office, that office, as it deals with a far greater number of articles, will be in a position to make up direct bags for a very much larger number of places, like Bombay, Cawnpore, Agra, Lucknow and Delhi, thereby saving labour in handling and sorting articles in the running sections. It is an axiom of the Post Office that no work should be thrown on a running section which can be performed in a stationary one, the expense being in the ratio of 3 to 1 in staff alone, not to mention the cost of haulage.

Concentration of sorting, although admirable for large towns, is not without its drawbacks. Where the system exists, postmasters are no longer answerable for the disposal of the outward mail, and they are unable to make any direct inquiry into public complaints regarding the loss or mis-sending of articles. As all the sorting is thrown on one mail office, it is necessary for the various post offices which serve it to close their mails sooner than they would if direct bags were prepared for the travelling sections, so that the latest time of posting has to be fixed at an earlier hour and the public suffer some inconvenience, especially in places remote from the station. A certain amount of double handling also occurs in towns with a large local delivery, in which case the mail has to be overhauled before despatch in order to pick out the local articles. Despite these drawbacks, the system is undoubtedly a good one whenever the postings of a number of offices can be concentrated in one mail office, but in small towns it is preferable for the post office to do its own sorting. Supervision is better, and the sorters can be used for other work. A solution of the difficulty might be found by placing the control of all the important through services under one Director of Mails with a few assistants to help him in supervision, and it has been suggested that probably the best results would be obtained if the Postmasters-General were responsible for both the sorting arrangements and the discipline of the staff upon all the railways within their circles. The present system of having different officers in charge of R.M.S. circles has caused a great deal of correspondence and not unfrequently means divided counsels. It has estranged the heads of postal circles from one of the most important branches of postal work, namely, the conveyance of mails by railway. At the same time, the Railway Mail Service work requires expert knowledge, and it is important that each railway should have to deal with only one man in the matter of the conveyance of mails within its system. This could not be done if Postmasters-General were in charge, as many railways pass through several postal circles. The question is full of difficulties, and after careful consideration it has been decided not to interfere with the existing arrangements, but to provide a closer co-ordination between the officers in charge of Railway Mail Service circles.

CHAPTER VII

MONEY ORDERS

PREVIOUS to 1880 the Money Order system of India was managed by the Government Treasuries. Bills of Exchange (Hundis) current for twelve months were issued by one treasury payable upon another, and as there were only 283 offices of issue and payment in the country the money order was not a popular means of remittance—in fact, it failed altogether to compete with the remittance of currency notes by post.

In 1878 Mr. Monteath, Director-General of the Post Office, proposed to Government to take over the money order business from the treasuries. He argued that, with the small number of treasuries and the trouble involved in reaching one of these every time a money order had to be sent or paid, the existing system could never become popular. The Post Office was able to provide 5500 offices of issue and payment, and the number of these would be always increasing and becoming more accessible to the people. Mr. Monteath's proposal was strongly opposed by the Comptroller-General, but was accepted by Government and sanctioned by the Secretary of State on the 27th November, 1879.

On the 1st January, 1880, the Post Office took over the whole management of issue and payment of money orders, and the audit was performed by the Compiler of Post

Office Accounts. For the purposes of money order work post offices were classified under four heads :

(1) Offices of issue.
(2) Offices of preparation.
(3) Offices of delivery.
(4) Offices of payment.

The office of preparation was always the head office of the district in which the addressee resided, and its duty was to prepare the money order in the name of the payee upon receipt of the intimation from the office of issue. The procedure was as follows : An application for a money order was made at the office of issue and, on payment of the amount with commission, a receipt was given to the remitter and the application was sent to the head office of the district in which the payee resided. This office was called the office of preparation, and if the payee resided in its delivery area it would also be both the office of delivery and payment. If, however, the payee resided at a sub or branch office, the office of preparation made out a money order for delivery at such sub or branch office and for payment at the post office named by the remitter in his application. It was not necessary for the office of delivery to be the office of payment ; the remitter could name any office authorized to pay money orders as the office of payment. Upon receipt of the money order by the payee an acknowledgment signed by him was sent to the remitter, and the payee had to make his own arrangements for cashing his money order at the proper office of payment.

The commission charged on money orders was accounted for by postage stamps affixed to the back of the application by the office of issue, and the rates were as follows:

	Rs.	A.	P.
Not exceeding Rs.10	0	2	0
Exceeding Rs. 10, but not exceeding Rs. 25	0	4	0
,, Rs. 25 ,, ,, Rs. 50	0	8	0
,, Rs. 50 ,, ,, Rs. 75	0	12	0
,, Rs. 75 ,, ,, Rs.100	1	0	0
,, Rs.100 ,, ,, Rs.125	1	4	0
,, Rs.125 ,, ,, Rs.150	1	8	0

Rs.150 was the maximum amount of a money order. Redirection was permissible, but such redirection did not affect the original office of payment, and this could only be altered by the payee signing the order and sending it to the office of preparation with an application for the issue of a new order payable to himself or anyone named by him at some specified office. A new order was issued, but a second commission was charged for this service. Money orders lapsed at the end of the month following that of issue, but were still payable for two months after lapsing if a second commission was paid; upon the expiry of that period they were forfeited to Government.

Certain special conditions with respect to money orders were (1) that not more than four could be issued to the same person by the same remitter in one day, except under special permission from the Compiler of Post Office Accounts, and (2) that under special orders the issue of money orders could be refused by any post office. Foreign money orders were granted on the United Kingdom, Canada, Germany, Belgium, Luxemburg, Heligoland, the Netherlands, Switzerland, Denmark and Italy.

The maximum amount was £10, and the rates of commission were:

	Rs.	A.	P.
Not exceeding £2	0	8	0
Exceeding £2, but not exceeding £5 .	1	0	0
" £5 " " £7 .	1	8	0
" £7 " " £10 .	2	0	0

For Canada the rates of commission were doubled.

In 1884 the Telegraphic Money Order system was introduced, with a charge of Rs.2 for the telegram exclusive of the money order commission upon the amount to be remitted. The charge was so high that it was thought safe to allow a money order up to Rs.600 in value to be sent by this means. The anomaly thus existed of having Rs.150 as the limit of an ordinary money order and Rs.600 as the limit of a telegraphic money order. The rule prohibiting more than four money orders daily being sent by the same remitter to the same payee, besides being quite unnecessary, proved no safeguard whatsoever. In actual practice the name of the remitter was not entered in the money order receipt, so that the post office of issue had no means of knowing how many money orders were sent by the same remitter, unless they were all presented at the same time. There was really no necessity to fix a low limit to the amount of a money order, as the whole procedure was quite different from that previously followed by the treasuries. The old treasury rule was that the amount of money orders issued in favour of one person in a district treasury must not exceed Rs.500 in one day, but then the money order was like a cheque payable to bearer and the paying treasury had no knowledge of the time at which it would be presented.

The Post Office, on the other hand, carried its own money orders and, if the office of payment was short of funds, it could hold back the money order until funds were obtained, and do so without the knowledge of the payee. These arguments prevailed, and in 1889 the restrictions were removed. The maximum value of an ordinary money order was raised to Rs.600, and no limit was placed upon the number which could be issued in favour of any one person. At the same time the rates were modified as follows :—

	Rs.	A.	P.
Not exceeding Rs.10	0	2	0
Exceeding Rs.10, but not exceeding Rs.25	0	4	0
Exceeding Rs.25—4 annas for each complete sum of 25 and 4 annas for the remainder, provided that, if the remainder did not exceed Rs.10, the charge would be 2 annas.			

On the 1st April, 1902, after a great deal of pressure from all classes of the community, Government reduced the commission upon a money order not exceeding Rs.5 to 1 anna.

The extension of the money order system to the payment of land revenue was first tried in the Benares Division of the North-West Provinces at the suggestion of Rai Bahadur Salig Ram, Postmaster-General, in the year 1884, and proved an immediate success. In eleven months, 13,914 land revenue money orders were sent, the gross value of which amounted to Rs.3,35,904. The system was a great advantage to small proprietors who lived at a distance from the Government Collecting

Stations. They found that the use of the ordinary money order for payment of revenue dues was not acceptable to the subordinate revenue officials, who suffered the loss of considerable perquisites thereby. Such remittances were generally refused on some pretext or other, either because they did not contain the correct amount due or else because the exact particulars required by the Land Revenue Department were not given on the money order form. To meet this difficulty a special form of money order was devised and the co-operation of District Collectors was invited. In 1886 the system was extended to the whole North-West Provinces except Kumaon, and a beginning was also made in ten districts of Bengal. The action of the Post Office was fully justified by results, and revenue money orders were quickly introduced into the Punjab, Central Provinces and Madras. In Madras they proved a failure, and were discontinued in 1892 after a three years' trial. The system was again introduced in 1906, but it still does not show any great signs of popularity, the figures for 1917–18 being 10,293 revenue money orders for Rs.1,29,400.

Rent money orders were first tried in the North-West Provinces in March, 1886; an experiment was also made in Bengal in October, 1886, and the system was extended to the Central Provinces in 1891. Except in parts of Bengal and the North-West Provinces, now known as the United Provinces, the payment of rent by money orders has never been popular, and the reason is not far to seek. Rent in India is usually in arrears and, whenever a tenant pays money to a zemindar (landholder), the latter can credit it against any portion of the arrears that he thinks fit. With a rent money order, the case is different, the money order itself and the receipt which has to be signed by the zemindar indicate exactly the period for which rent is being paid, and to that period it must be devoted. This is the ordinary ruling of the rent courts and does not at all meet the wishes of zemindars who want to have their tenants in their power. Besides this important factor, there is the rooted objection of all subordinates, whether they be government servants or zemindars' agents, to be deprived of the time-honoured offerings which all self-respecting tenants should make to the landlord's servants at the time of paying their rents, and the appearance of a postman with a sheaf of money orders, however punctual the payments may be, is hardly an adequate substitute for the actual attendance of the tenants themselves.

In 1886 the plan of paying money orders at the houses of payees was adopted and proved very satisfactory. India was indebted to Germany for the idea, which not only conferred a great boon on the public but tended to reduce the accumulations of cash at post offices and to accelerate the closure of money order accounts.

In Appendix " E " is given the number and value of inland money orders issued in India from 1880–81 to 1917–18, and the steady increase from year to year is a certain sign of the great public need which the Indian money order system satisfies, and of the confidence that is placed in it.

On the 1st October, 1884, the public was given the opportunity of employing the telegraph for the transmission of inland money orders, and during the first six months of the scheme 5788 money orders for Rs.3,75,000 were issued. The cost of Rs.2 for the telegram and $\frac{1}{2}$ per cent for money order commission was a decided bar to the popularity of the telegraphic money order, which at first was chiefly used in Burma and Madras owing to the isolated positions of those provinces. In 1887 the Post Office relinquished its commission on orders for sums not exceeding Rs.10, and the telegraph charge was reduced to R.1. This led to an immediate increase of traffic, the number of such orders in 1887–88 being 45,417 compared with 18,540 in the previous year, more than half of which were issued from Burma. In 1917–18 the total number of telegraphic money orders issued was 875,000 and the value Rs.6,22,00,000 of which about three-fifths came from Burma. With the improvements in railway communication in India which are continually taking place, the pre-eminence of Burma in the matter of telegraphic money orders is likely to continue owing to her isolation and the largely expanding trade of Rangoon.

The ubiquitous swindler was not long in taking advantage of the telegraphic money order to ply a profitable trade. His chief resorts are Benares, Rameswaram, Tripati and the other great places of pilgrimage in India; his victim is generally some unfortunate pilgrim, who is only too anxious to meet an obliging friend willing to act as a guide and adviser in one of the sacred cities, and the procedure adopted is always the same. The swindler acts the part of the kind stranger and finds out all the details of the pilgrim's family. He then goes to the local post office, represents himself to be the pilgrim and sends a telegram to his victim's relations to say that he has lost his money and wants a certain sum at once. So confiding are the people of India that it is very seldom that a request of this kind does not meet with an immediate response, and the swindler, by waiting a couple of days during which he takes good care to ingratiate himself with the post office officials, walks off the richer by a considerable amount. The earlier reports of the Post Office on the telegraphic money order system abound in cases of the kind, and very stringent measures were adopted to put a stop to the practice. Identification of payees by well-known residents of the neighbourhood was insisted upon, and a payee of a telegraphic money order had to prove his claim and give satisfactory evidence of his permanent address. Despite all precautions, the telegraphic money order swindler is still common enough and manages to get away with large sums from time to time.

Probably in no country in the world is the poor man so dependent upon the Post Office for the transmission of small sums of money as in India. The average value of an inland money order in 1917–18 was Rs.18, and it is not infrequent for amounts as small as Rs.5 to be sent by telegraphic money order. The reason undoubtedly is the facility with which payment is made and the absolute confidence which the Indian villager places in the Post Office. An Indian coolie in Burma, who has saved a few hundred rupees and wants to return to his village, seldom carries the money on his person, and he has a strange mistrust for banks; they are much too grand places for him to enter. He usually goes to a post office and sends to himself a money order addressed to the post office nearest his own home and then he is satisfied. It may be months before he turns up to claim the money, as he frequently gets a job on the way back or spends some time at a place of pilgrimage, but he knows that his money is safe enough and he is quite content to use the Post Office as a temporary bank to the great inconvenience of the Audit Office. It is not too much to say that the money order system of India is part and parcel of the life of the people. They use it to assist their friends and defy their enemies. They have in that magic slip of paper, the money order acknowledgment, what they never had before, that which no number of lying witnesses can disprove, namely, an indisputable proof of payment.

CHAPTER VIII

SAVINGS BANK

THE first Government Savings Banks were opened at the three Presidency towns of Calcutta, Madras and Bombay in 1833, 1834 and 1835, respectively. These Banks were announced as intended for the investment of the savings of "all classes British and Native," the return of the deposits with interest being guaranteed by Government. Between 1863 and 1865 the management of the Savings Banks was transferred to the Presidency Banks, and each Presidency framed its own rules. The first deposits were limited to Rs.500, and upon the balance reaching this sum it was invested in a Government Loan. The limit was gradually increased to Rs.3000 with interest at 4 per cent, but, as it was found that many people deposited the maximum amount at once, a rule was brought in prohibiting the deposit of more than Rs.500 a year in any one account.

In 1870 District Savings Banks were instituted in all parts of India except Calcutta and the Presidencies of Madras and Bombay. The limits for deposits were fixed at Rs.500 a year with a total of Rs.3000 and interest at 3¾ per cent was fixed. In December, 1879, revised rules were drawn up for District and other Government Savings Banks, the most important change being that the limit of a deposit account was raised to Rs.5000 and interest was fixed at $4\frac{1}{6}$ per cent. The result of these rules was to attract to the Savings Banks a large number of deposits which should have gone to other banks, and in 1880 the monthly limit of Rs.500 with a maximum of Rs.3000 was again imposed and interest was reduced to $3\frac{3}{4}$ per cent.

The proposal to establish Post Office Savings Banks on the lines of those which existed in England met with great opposition, especially from the Comptroller-General. The same arguments were brought forward which the opponents of the Post Office Savings Bank Bill in England used when Mr. Gladstone managed to get this wise and beneficial measure through both Houses in 1861. In 1882 the first Post Office Savings Banks were opened in every part of India except Calcutta, Bombay and the head-quarter stations of Madras. In Madras, savings banks could be opened by the Director-General, provided they were not within five miles of a head-quarter station. The immediate consequence of this measure was an increase in the number of savings banks in the country from 197 to 4243. The minimum deposit was fixed at 4 annas, and interest was allowed at 3 pies a month on every complete sum of Rs.5; it was also arranged to purchase Government Securities for depositors. The end of the first year's working showed 39,121 depositors with a balance of Rs.27,96,796.

On the 1st April, 1886, District Savings Banks were abolished and the balances transferred to the Post Office, but the Local Government Savings Banks at Calcutta, Bombay and Madras remained in the hands of the Presidency Banks until the 1st October, 1896.

In 1904, when the balance at the credit of depositors exceeded 130 millions of rupees, the Government of

India began to be rather nervous of being liable to pay up such a large sum at call without any warning. A sudden rush of depositors to withdraw their savings would tax the resources of Government to the utmost and, in order to afford some protection, a rule was made that an extra quarter per cent would be paid upon deposits, which were not liable to withdrawal until six months' notice had been given. Needless to say, the bait did not prove attractive. The additional interest meant practically nothing to small depositors and was poor compensation to large depositors for the inconvenience of having their money tied up for six months. What the measure did involve was a great increase of work and account-keeping for little or no purpose, as the number of accounts subject to six months' notice of withdrawal never exceeded 3 per cent of the total. These accounts were abolished in 1908 and, although the Government of India does not keep any special reserve against the balance in the Post Office Savings Bank, the depositor has the satisfaction of knowing that his deposit is guaranteed by the whole revenue of the country.

The history of the Post Office Savings Bank in India is rather monotonous. With a single exception it has been one of continual prosperity and expansion from 1882, the year of its commencement, to 1914. The balance on the 31st March, 1914, was over 231 million rupees, and, as the money belongs very largely to small depositors, who can demand immediate payment, the bank is placed in a very responsible position towards the public. It will, therefore, be of advantage to examine the political and economic crises which have occurred in this period, and how they have affected the small depositors' confidence in the Government of India.

In Appendix D is given the number of accounts and the balance year by year from 1882 to 1914, which shows that in no year have the accounts failed to increase in number and only in 1897–8 has the balance at the credit of depositors declined. Yet during this period three important crises occurred. The first was in 1885, and was known as the Russian Scare, the second in 1896–7 when India was visited by the worst famine on record, and the third in 1907–8 when a great wave of sedition and discontent spread over the country.

Two of these crises were political and one economic, and it is a remarkable fact that the effect of the former two was felt almost entirely, and of the latter very largely, in the Bombay Presidency. This circumstance goes to prove that the inhabitants of Bombay are more in touch with the affairs of the world than those in other parts of India.

The Russian Scare of 1885, culminating in the "Penjdeh Affair," led to very heavy withdrawals from almost all the more important savings banks on the Bombay side. No less than Rs.2,93,000 were paid out to depositors in the Presidency Savings Bank from the 1st to the 22nd April. The withdrawals in March from Ahmedabad, Kaira, Broach and Surat totalled Rs.2,80,000 against Rs.1,10,000 in March, 1884, and the excess of withdrawals over deposits for the whole Presidency in January, February and March amounted to Rs.9,50,000. The rest of India was not affected by the scare, in fact the total number of Savings Bank accounts increased by 38,000 and the balances by Rs.59,00,000 despite the heavy deficit in Bombay.

The crisis of 1897 was purely economic and was due to a widespread famine and abnormally high prices. Its effect was felt in the Savings Bank for three years, the balance falling from Rs.9,63,00,000 in 1896–7 to Rs. 9,28,00,000 in 1897–8, and not reaching Rs.9,64,00,000 until 1899–00. The Bombay Postal Circle accounted for Rs.30,50,000 out of the Rs.35,00,000 deficit in India, the other deficits being in Madras, the North-West Provinces and Oudh, and Bengal.

In 1907–8, as I have already mentioned, the country was full of unrest. Leaflets calling on the men to mutiny were being distributed broadcast among the Indian regiments. Several Sikh regiments were supposed to be seriously disaffected. The feeling in Bengal against the British Government was being carefully nurtured, but the real head-quarters of the anti-British movement was Poona. In 1908–9 the balance of the Savings Bank increased by Rs.5,00,000 only, which meant a serious set-back considering the way in which the Post Office was developing, but the figures for the Bombay Postal Circle are peculiarly instructive. The number of accounts actually increased from 264,558 to 271,604, whereas the balance at the credit of depositors declined from Rs.4,41,00,000 to Rs. 4,30,00,000, the actual decrease being Rs.11,46,388. Now in this year Bengal showed an increase of nearly Rs.2,00,000, and the decline in the proportional rate of increase in India was found to be due to the heavy withdrawals of some depositors in Bombay. There is reason to believe that a number of wealthy persons belonging to the commercial class use the Post Office Savings Bank in Bombay as a convenient place to deposit money. This class of depositors numbered 12,198 in 1907–08 and 12,503 in

1908–09, which is larger than in Bengal. Such people do not deposit their money from motives of saving or thrift, but merely take advantage of the convenience which the Post Office offers as a safe place to keep, at interest, money which can be immediately realized. The rule which permits a depositor to have accounts in his own behalf or on behalf of any minor relatives or any minor of whom he happens to be the guardian has opened a way to great abuse of the system. There is nothing to prevent a man having any number of imaginary relatives and opening accounts in all their names. He can deposit the maximum in each account, and naturally in times of crisis or when money is tight the Savings Bank has to face the immediate withdrawal of all these amounts. As one example of what is done, a case came to light some years ago in which a depositor at Dharwar was authorized to operate on eighty-three accounts with a balance of nearly Rs.30,000. He was a broker by profession and it was quite possible for him to control a balance of Rs.2,00,000 in the Post Office, if he wished to do so. Further inquiries made at the time elicited that one depositor at Bijapur controlled forty-two accounts, another at Surat thirty, and another at Karwar nineteen. Such persons are really speculators and are a danger to the Savings Bank, and it would be interesting to know what proportion they hold of the total deposits in the Bombay Circle. These deposits represent a very high proportion of the total in India, so that the action of any strong body of depositors in Bombay has a very serious effect on the balance of the Savings Bank.

The examination of transactions for the thirty years previous to 1914 has this satisfactory result that, with the exception of the undesirable element in Bombay, a political crisis, at any rate, seems to have no marked influence upon the great mass of depositors in India. The number of depositors on the 31st March, 1914, was 1,638,725 with a balance of Rs.23,16,75,000. The outbreak of the war with Germany, however, had a disastrous effect on the Savings Bank balances. When the announcement was made that the German Government had temporarily confiscated the Savings Bank deposits in that country, a regular panic ensued and within a few months about 100 millions of rupees were withdrawn. The action of the Government of India, however, in meeting all claims in full did a great deal to allay public fears, and a certain amount of money came back later in the year, but the balance on the 31st March, 1915, had declined from about 231 to 149 millions of rupees. Since then there has been a gradual recovery, and the balance on the 31st March, 1918, was nearly 166 million rupees. The recovery would have been much quicker but for the large sale of five-year cash certificates in 1917–18 on behalf of the War Loan. The price received was about 100 million rupees, of which a considerable portion was withdrawn from Savings Bank deposits. At the same time the small depositors were busy purchasing cash certificates with money that would otherwise have been put into the Post Office Savings Bank. Now that the War is over and the rush for cash certificates has ceased, there is every prospect that the Post Office Savings Bank will shortly regain its former popularity.

CHAPTER IX

THE PEOPLE AND THE POST OFFICE

THERE is no branch of the Public Service that comes into such close contact with the people as the Post Office. Its officials are consulted in all kinds of family troubles, they have to deal with curious superstitions and beliefs and to overcome the prejudices ingrained by an hereditary system of caste. The official measure of the successful working of the Department is gauged by the annual statistics, but the real measure of its success may be learned from the attitude of the people themselves. The Indian villager dreads the presence of the Government officer in his neighbourhood, but he makes an exception in the case of Post Office employés. The postman is always a welcome visitor and, if he fails to attend regularly, a complaint is invariably made.

It is in the delivery of correspondence throughout the smaller towns and rural tracts in India that the Post Office has to face some of its most difficult problems. Towns in India, with the exception of the Presidency and more important towns, are mere collections of houses, divided into "mohullas" or quarters. Few streets have names, and consequently addresses tend to be vague descriptions which tax all the ingenuity of the delivery agents. Among the poorer classes definite local habitations with names are almost unknown, and the best that a correspondent can do is to give the name of the addressee, his trade and the bazaar that he frequents. Such cases are comparatively simple, as the postman is usually a man with an intimate knowledge of the quarter, and the recipients of letters have no objection to be described by their physical defects, such as "he with the lame leg" or "the squint eye" or "the crooked back"! Real difficulties, however, arise when articles are addressed to members of the peripatetic population consisting of pilgrims, boatmen and other wanderers. There is an enormous boat traffic on the large rivers of Bengal and Burma. The boat is the home of a family, it wanders over thousands of miles of channels carrying commodities, and letters to the owner rarely give anything except a general direction to deliver the article on board a boat carrying wood or rice from some river port to another. The pilgrims who travel from shrine to shrine in the country are also a puzzle to the Post Office, and in sacred places, like Benares, special postmen have to be trained to deliver their letters.

The forms of address are seldom very helpful for a speedy distribution and delivery of the mail. The following are characteristic of what a sorter has to deal with any day:—

"With good blessings to the fortunate Babu Kailas Chandra Dey, may the dear boy live long. The letter to go to the Baidiabati post office. The above-named person will get it on reaching Baidiabati, Khoragachi, Goynapara. (Bearing.)"

"To the one inseparable from my heart, the fortunate Babu Sibnath Ghose, having the same heart as mine. From post office Hasnabad to the village of Ramnathpur, to reach the house of the fortunate

Babu Prayanath Ghose, District Twenty-four Parganas. Don't deliver this letter to any person other than the addressee, Mr. Postman. This my request to you."

"If the Almighty pleases, let this envelope, having arrived at the city of Calcutta in the neighbourhood of Kulutola, at the counting house of Sirajudin and Alladad Khan, merchants, be offered to and read by the happy light of my eyes of virtuous manners and beloved of the heart, Mian Sheikh Inayat Ali, may his life be long! Written on the tenth of the blessed Ramzan in the year 1266 of the Hejira of our Prophet, and despatched as bearing. Having without loss of time paid the postage and received the letter, you will read it. Having abstained from food and drink, considering it forbidden to you, you will convey yourself to Jaunpur and you will know this to be a strict injunction."

The three addresses given below have been taken from letters posted by Hindus to Hindus, and it will be noticed that they merely bear the names of persons with no indication of the place of delivery.

"To the sacred feet of the most worshipful, the most respected brother, Guru Pershad Singh!"

"To his Highness the respected brother, beneficent lord of us the poor, my benefactor, Munshi Manik Chand."

"To the blessed feet of the most worshipful younger uncle, Kashi Nath Banerji."

It is not uncommon for Europeans to receive letters with honorific titles added to their names, in fact it would be considered impolite to address an English gentleman in the vernacular by his mere name. Such a thing is never done. Whatever address is given by the writer, the Indian postman has his special methods of noting it. He seldoms knows English, and when names are read out to him by the delivery clerk he scrawls his own description on the back in a script that can only be read by himself. A well-known judge of the Calcutta High Court, Sir John Stevens, was much amused to find that the words "Old Stevens Sahib" were constantly written in the vernacular on the back of his letters, this being done to distinguish him from his younger colleague, Mr. Justice Stephens.

A story recently received from the Persian Gulf explains how it is that letters sometimes fail to reach their destinations despite the greatest care on the part of the Post Office. The incident is worthy of the *Arabian Nights*, and I will quote the account given by the sub-postmaster of Linga.

"On the 8th of December in the year 1912 a well-known merchant of Linga, Aga Abbasalli by name, informed me that his agents at Bombay, Karachi and other places in India had informed him by telegraph that for the last two weeks they had received no mails from him. He asked for an explanation from me for this, indirectly holding me responsible and even threatening to report me to you, for he maintained that the letters he sent to the Post for many years past had, at least, always reached their destination, if late, and that he could not now for his life imagine as to how it was that the several letters which he himself sent to the Post, by bearer, for the last two weeks, were lost during transmission. As Abbasalli was known to me, I sent word to him through somebody to the effect that, in the first place, he would do well to examine the bearer with whom he sent his letters to the Post. The bearer was thereupon called by him and confronted with the question of his mails; but before quoting the silly dolt's interesting reply it would be better to note the following few points:—

There are two identical terms in Persian, the "Poos" and the "Poost," which have three distinct meanings, the word "Poos" meaning a dock, or, in such a place as the port of Linga, only a shelter for ships' anchorage, whilst the word "Poost" meaning (1) hides and skins, or leather and (2) the Post Office. As far as pronunciations are concerned it has been a very indiscriminate colloquialism at Linga to pronounce both the above said words alike as "Poos," without any regard to the final "t" of the word "Poost"; and practically, therefore, the word "Poos" has three separate meanings as quoted above. The "Poost-e-Buzurg" or the "Poos-e-Buzurg," literally equal to the big Post Office, is used by the mass of people for the British Post Office at Linga, as distinct from the Persian Post Office, which is known as the "Poost-e-Ajam." But to many again the "Poos-e-Buzurg" is known as the big dock, also styled the "Poos-e-Aga Bedar" (Aga Bedar's dock), in contradistinction from another which is smaller, and is only known as the "Poos-e-Bazar," that is, the Bazar dock. Moreover, both the big dock and the British Post Office are situated somewhere near Aga Bedar's Coffee shop, the latter being, however, a little farther than the dock.

Having noted these points I now beg to revert to the question put to his bearer by Abbasalli and the former's reply thereto. "What did you do with my mails, that

I gave you, for the last two weeks, to be conveyed to the 'Poost'?" asks Abbasalli in his vernacular, and the bearer replies, "The first week when you told me to carry your letters to the 'Poost' I *went* to the shoemaker's and was putting them *exactly* amongst the 'Poost' (meaning leather and leather-ware), as ordered by you, but, he won't let me do so, and said I should carry the letters to the 'Poos-e-Buzurg' near Aga Bedar's Coffee shop." "Ah! you blockhead, you," explained the exasperated merchant, "but, what did you do with my letters after all when he told you to carry them to the 'Poos-e-Buzurg'?" "Why, rest easy on the point," says the bearer, "I carried them exactly to the 'Poos-e-Buzurg' (meaning the big dock) and threw the letters in. The first time when there was plenty of water in the dock (on account of tide) I had simply to throw your letters in, and I am sure they must have reached their destination quite all right; but the next week, when there was but little water in the dock, I had to dig a pit in the sand to put the mails in, and perhaps they may not have reached their destination."

Poor Abbasalli was quite perplexed and awfully sorry to know that all the valuable letters written by him for the two weeks, some containing cheques even, as I am given to understand, were thus entirely washed away by the merciless waves; but, no less embarrassed am I, on hearing of the tomfoolery, to think of what blame it may sometimes accidentally and unnecessarily entail on a Postmaster, and I therefore venture to put this real story before you, with the fullest hope that, in future, complaints of a like nature may kindly be considered only on their due merits.

I may be allowed to add that the story was related by

me before H.B.M.'s Vice-Consul and the small European Community at the Linga Club, and they all, while sympathizing with me in my perplexity, enjoyed a hearty laugh over the recital.

On the 31st March, 1918, there were over 19,410 post offices and 49,749 letter boxes in India to serve a population of 319 million people in an area of 1,622,000 square miles. This gives a post office to about every 16,000 persons, or to each 83 square miles of country, which seems a very poor service by comparison with Western countries, but, when one considers that the literate population of India is only 18,500,000, the service is good and the prospect of future development with the increase of education is enormous.

It must not be supposed, however, that the Post Office confines its energies to the literate population. It is largely used by people who can neither read nor write, and this is made possible by the existence of professional letter-writers, who are to be found in every town and village in the country. For a pice (farthing) they will write an address, and for two pice they will write a short letter or a postcard or fill up a money order, though slightly higher fees are charged if the letter is very long.

In rural tracts where it is not worth while to maintain a post office, the people are served by a letter-box or by a village postman who makes periodical visits and acts as a travelling post office. It is a wonderful achievement of the Department that there is scarcely a village in India which does not lie within the beat of a village postman. The competition between villages to obtain post offices is often very keen, and a Postmaster-General has many a troublesome decision to make, as to which of two or three neighbouring villages is to have the honour conferred upon it. While the matter is yet undecided the competitors vie with each other in pouring correspondence into the nearest post office in order to show the postal importance of their respective villages, an importance which is apt to decline sadly when once the post office has been opened. On one occasion, when Postmaster-General, I received application from two villages A and B for the opening of post offices. There happened to be an office in a village C close by, but the applications stated that this village was separated from them by a river, difficult to cross at most seasons and quite impossible during the rains. The inspector who visited the locality reported that the river could be crossed dry-shod at most seasons and with little difficulty during the monsoon, but that A was a much more important place than C and that the post office ought to be transferred there. A fresh complication was then started, and the indignation of the villagers in C knew no bounds. They threatened to carry the matter up to the Viceroy, and for the time they began to post enough letters to justify the existence of an office in the village. The dispute was finally settled by establishing an office at A in addition to the one at C, on condition that one or the other would be closed if the postal work done did not justify its continuance.

One of the most important duties of a Superintendent is to watch carefully the work of village postmen. Statistics are kept regularly of the articles delivered and collected by them, and these statistics give a very true indication of the places where new post offices are required in rural tracts. In this way the Department keeps in touch with the whole country, and a special grant has been allowed by Government for opening experimental offices in places which show signs of needing permanent ones. An experimental office is opened for a period of six months and, if it leads to a development of correspondence and pays its way, it is made permanent at the end of that time, but unless it is a complete failure the experiment is extended up to two years in order to give the people of the neighbourhood every chance of retaining the office. This policy has been most successful and has taught the village people that they are largely responsible for the maintenance of their own post offices. The postmaster is invariably a local man, either the village schoolmaster or a shop-keeper, who gets a small salary, which, combined with the dignity of His Majesty's mails, gives him a direct interest in making the office a profitable concern.

The annual statistics of the Post Office serve as a barometer of the prosperity of India. The Department has entered into the lives of the people with its lines of communication, its savings bank, money orders, payment of pensions and sale of quinine. It has only one aim and that aim is recognized by all, namely, to do the greatest good for the greatest number.

CHAPTER X

THE INDIAN POSTMAN

THE conditions under which postal articles in England and India are delivered differ so vastly that a knowledge of Indian life is necessary in order to understand the difficulties that lie in the way of good delivery work in this country. The smart official walking four miles an hour and shooting the contents of his satchel into every house on his beat with a rat-a-tat is unknown. House doors in India have no knockers and no letter-boxes, and among the better class inhabitants, both European and Indian, it is customary to send messengers to the post office to fetch the unregistered mail, so that to this extent the postman's work is reduced. The balance of the articles received by him often forms a strange medley in many languages, of which perhaps he is able to read one with difficulty. In a large town like Calcutta letters are received addressed in as many as a dozen different languages, and special clerks versed in the various tongues have to be employed. Luckily people of the same race are accustomed to congregate in the same quarters of the town, and the postmen are able to get some of the local residents to assist them in deciphering many a doubtful address. In Bombay certain private delivery agencies exist, which are recognized by the Department and which work very satisfactorily. On the whole the distribution of letters to the public is performed in a leisurely fashion which is quite in accordance with the national character. One may often see a postman, with the assistance of a dozen of the literate inhabitants of the quarter, spelling out from a dirty piece of folded paper an address, which turns out to be one Gunga Din living near the temple of Hanuman in the courtyard of some ancient who has died years ago, but whose name is still perpetuated in the soil where his house once stood. Gunga Din may be dead or vanished, the quarter knows him no more, but his sister's grand-nephew arrives to take the letter, and after some haggling agrees to pay the 1 anna due on it, for such letters are invariably sent bearing. This little episode being finished the postman proceeds on his beat to find another enigmatical addressee, and is it any wonder that, although his salary is often a low one, the Indian postman is one of the most expensive delivery agents in the world? He seldom delivers more than three hundred articles a day, and in the Indian business quarters of the town he gets rid of the majority of these at the post office door, since the merchants and others who expect letters always waylay the postman just as he is proceeding on his beat, knowing well that it may be many hours before he will find it convenient to visit them at their houses.

In the matter of slow delivery, however, the public are more frequently to blame for delays than the postman, especially in the case of articles which have to be signed for. Parcels, money orders or registered letters are taken at the door by a servant and, if the sahib is at his bath or busy, there is a long and tedious wait before the signed receipts are brought back. It is extraordinary how callous people are in this respect

COMBINED PASSENGER AND MAIL MOTOR VAN. KANGRA VALLEY SERVICE

towards the interests of the Post Office and their own neighbours, while they are always ready to complain if the smallest delay or mistake occurs to any articles for themselves. It can be easily understood that where such conditions prevail, and that is all over India, fast delivery is impossible, and the very best regulations for getting the men quickly to their beats are useless when they are detained unnecessarily at every house.

In India most money orders are paid at the door by postmen, and in towns, where there are large payments to be made, special sets of postmen are employed for the purpose. The rules regarding the payment of money orders are very strict and, when the payees are not well-known persons, identification by a respectable resident is insisted upon. In large pilgrim resorts, like Benares, where the pilgrims are continually getting remittances and are necessarily unknown, there is a special class of professional identifiers, consisting chiefly of the innkeepers. These men for a small fee are always ready to swear to the identity of any pilgrim for whom a money order has arrived, and, strange to say, they are often ready to pay up if it is found that their identification was incorrect and that the money was paid to the wrong person, a not unfrequent occurrence.

The postman, however, has to bear the brunt in case of the identification not being complete, and his responsibility in the matter is great. The convenience to the public of having their money brought to their doors is considerable, but it is a source of continual anxiety and expense to the Post Office. Large sums of money are entrusted daily to men on small pay. When the limit, which a postman is allowed to take, is exceeded, an overseer has to accompany him on his beat. Accounts have to be kept with each of the money order postmen and must be settled before the day's cash can be closed. Complaints of short payment are frequent and necessitate detailed inquiries with usually very unsatisfactory results, while the opportunities for blackmail are unlimited. Despite these drawbacks, it would now be scarcely possible to revert to a system by which everyone who received a money order was obliged to take payment of it at a post office, although greater security for both the public and the Department would be gained thereby. In certain parts of the country rural delivery is effected with extraordinary difficulty. On the North-West frontier the village postman goes in danger of his life from trans-border tribesmen. In the forest tracts of Central India the attacks of man-eating tigers are not merely travellers' tales, but grim realities. In the riverine districts of Eastern Bengal the postman has to go from village to village by boat, and a storm on one of these immense rivers is a bad thing to face in a frail canoe. Nor is the boat journey the worst trouble; a long tramp from the bank through swampy rice and jute fields is often the only way to a village which has to be visited twice a week. It is no wonder that the village postman sometimes takes the easiest way of delivering his letters by going to the most important place in his beat on market day; for, if he cannot find the actual addressees there, he is pretty sure to find some people from the vicinity who are willing to take charge of their neighbours' correspondence, but often not too careful about delivering it. Hence the origin of much trouble, complaints and hard swearing. Half a dozen witnesses are always forthcoming to affirm that the postman visited the village *in propria persona* on that particular day, and to prove it the visit book with the signature of one of the perjurers is produced. How can the mere negative evidence of another half-dozen stand against these convincing proofs?

On the Malabar side of the peninsula, where a very strict form of Brahminism prevails, persons of low caste are forbidden to enter the quarters of a town occupied by Brahmins, and care has to be taken to place these quarters in the beats of high caste postmen. In Palghat there was almost a riot on one occasion when a postman of inferior caste attempted to enter a Brahmin street in the performance of his duties, and the Postmaster-General was promptly called to order by the indignant inhabitants. It was nearly a question whether he should be fined and compelled to feed a thousand beggars in accordance with the custom of the caste, but, on proving that he was an indigent member of the Indian Civil Service with a wife and family in England, he was pardoned on admitting his error and promising that no repetition of the offence should occur.

As a rule the Indian postman is reasonably honest and, if not interfered with at an unseasonable moment by an over-zealous inspector, his accounts will come out square in the course of time. The maintenance of a private debit account with the Department at the expense of the payees of money orders is not unknown. The usual practice is to withhold the payment of a certain number of money orders for a few days and to use the money for some profitable speculation, such as cotton gambling or betting on the opium sales. Recently one of the most respected postmen in the Big Bazaar of Calcutta was found to have overreached himself in carrying out this policy. He was on a very heavy money order beat, and used regularly to keep back a number of money orders and forge the payees' receipts so as to satisfy the office that payment had been made. He kept a private account of these, and when he decided to pay any one whose money had been withheld he filled up a blank form, of which plenty are always available, and took the payee's signature on this. The practice continued for some time and, as everyone got paid in turn and the postman was a most plausible fellow, no complaints were made. At last his speculations went wrong, he got into very deep water and an unpleasant person complained to the postmaster that he had not received a money order which he knew to have been sent weeks before. This led to an inquiry, and the postman, being caught unawares, was unable to account for about 17,000 rupees' worth of money orders due to various people in the city.

One of the great problems of the Post Office in large towns is to arrange deliveries and beats of postmen so that people will get their letters in the shortest time after the arrival of the mail trains. It used to be thought that the best way to effect this purpose was to have several delivery centres in order that postmen might be near their beats and the waste of time in walking to the beats be avoided. To enable this to be done, the Railway Mail Service was expected to sort all postal articles into separate bags for the different delivery offices. The principle is excellent in theory, but in practice it has not worked well and has led to indiscriminate missending to wrong delivery offices. For instance, Madras at one time had twenty-six delivery offices and, if people could have been induced to address their correspondence to one of these offices with the word (Madras) in brackets underneath, there might have been some hope of it being properly sorted by the Railway Mail Service, but probably 80 per cent of articles were simply addressed to Madras with or without the name of a street, so that the sorters were set an impossible task and the General Post Office had to maintain a special staff for sorting and conveying such letters to the offices from which they would eventually be delivered. The present policy is to have as few delivery offices as possible, and to have postmen conveyed to more distant beats. This has proved far more satisfactory ; it relieves the work in the R.M.S., enables the postmen to be kept under better control and reduces the possibility of articles going astray.

While working at the best arrangements for delivery at Calcutta Mr. Owens, late Presidency Postmaster, devised the system of what is known for want of a better name as "continuous delivery." Every beat is provided with a locked box placed in a shop or some suitable place in the beat, and the letters for delivery are placed in this box by messengers sent direct from the post office. The postman goes straight to his beat and remains on duty there for six hours, he finds his letters in the box and is supposed to make the complete round of his beat every hour, delivering articles and clearing the pillar boxes *en route*. When he returns to the locked box he finds a fresh consignment of letters for delivery, and deposits those that he has collected for despatch, to be taken away by the messenger on his next visit. The system is a good one and has worked well. It saves labour and, if the beats are properly supervised and the postmen work conscientiously, a great quickening up of delivery is effected. If, however, supervision is at all lax, human nature asserts itself, postmen are inclined to loiter and they allow letters to accumulate so that one round can be made to do the work of two. Owing to the difficulty of supervision, the continuous delivery system has not many ardent supporters in the Post Office at the present time.

The postman is, in fine, one of the most important factors in the Department, and upon his energy and honesty much depends. It therefore behoves the authorities to see that a good class of man is recruited. In addition to being able to read and write the language of that part of the country in which he serves, he should know enough English to be able to read addresses easily, but in order to obtain this class of man careful recruitment is necessary and a good initial salary with reasonable prospects of promotion must be given. Much has been done in recent years to improve the status of postmen and all branch postmasterships, which are not held by extra-departmental agents, are now open to them. This is a great step forward. The Department used to be very parsimonious in the matter of uniforms, and in many important offices postmen had to pay for them themselves. Nor was there any uniformity even in each circle about the uniforms supplied by Government. In one town red coats and blue turbans were seen, in another blue coats and red turbans, in another khaki coats and nondescript turbans, while the men who supplied themselves with uniform presented at times the most extraordinary appearance. The pattern of postmen's uniform has now been standardized for each circle, and uniforms are supplied free of cost in all head offices and large sub-offices. Warm clothing is also given in all places with a cold climate. There is no doubt about the value of a uniform to a postman. It adds a certain amount of dignity to him and, like the soldier, he is the better man for having a distinctive badge of office. The pay has recently been greatly improved and much has been done to ameliorate conditions under which they serve. There are over 27,000 postmen in India; the interests of these men are identical with those of the Department, and their welfare should be the aim of every postal officer.

CHAPTER XI

POST OFFICE BUILDINGS

"I DON'T think" was the terse though somewhat vulgar reply of a well-known district officer on the western side of India when asked if he would like to have a post office erected in a conspicuous place at the head-quarters of his district. He was willing to give the site in question for a clock tower, a public library or even a statue of one of his predecessors, but a post office, "No, thank you." The reason for this attitude may be easily understood by those who have seen the ordinary Indian post office of a few years ago. It used generally to be a rented building quite unsuited for the purpose and made perfectly hideous by small additions and projections constructed from time to time in order to meet demands for increased space. The windows and doors were used not for light and air nor even for giving access to the interior, but for business purposes. They were blocked up with the exception of a small hole just the size of a pane of glass, through which the members of the public had to try to get a clerk to attend to their requirements. When a Government building existed it was very little better, except in the matter of repairs. The interior of the ordinary post office was a dreadful sight a few years ago, a mass of untidy tables, a large number of cupboards, known in India as almirahs, ill-designed sorting cases and dirt, this last article being the most prevalent everywhere. Letters were sorted on the floor for convenience, and the delivery table with its ragged occupants, who did duty for postmen, was a sight for the gods.

The position of a post office in a town is a matter of the first importance, but the chief object of the authorities in the early days of the Imperial Post Office seems to have been economy. As a building in a back street naturally costs less than one in a main street, many of the city offices are hidden away in the most inaccessible slums. It is, indeed, a case of Mohamed and the mountain, and the Post Office, secure in its monopoly, was not going to afford any unnecessary conveniences to its clients. Many of my readers will doubtless recall some of those upstairs offices in big cities, which do an enormous amount of work, especially in the afternoon, the approach being a single staircase just broad enough for one person to ascend. Imagine the turmoil at the busy hours of the day. In Bara Bazar, Calcutta, and Benares City, two famous instances which come to mind at the moment, where there is a heavy despatch of parcels, the confined space round the parcel windows was the scene of a petty riot every afternoon. Such a state of affairs could not exist for a month in a country where the better class of people perform their own post office business; unfortunately in India all this kind of work is done by native messengers who are not particular about the surroundings of an office and usually have plenty of time to spare. Things, however, improved in recent years under the direction of Sir Arthur Fanshawe and Sir Charles Stewart-Wilson, both of whom had the critical faculty strongly developed. Assisted by the genius of Mr. James Begg, Consulting Architect to the Government of India, they have done much to improve the modern post office, with the result that the Department now has some really fine buildings. For beauty of design the new Bombay General Post Office, completed in 1910, is one of the finest in the East. The reproduction of it in this book gives but little idea of its splendid proportions, and its internal structure has been planned with a view to facilitate postal work and to allow for future expansion.

The General Post Office in Calcutta was built in 1868 from designs made by Mr. Granville, Architect to the Government of India. The site is of great historical interest owing to its association with the tragedy of the Black Hole of Calcutta. The building is hardly large enough now for the great mass of work which it has to transact and, although the removal of the Postmaster-General's Office and the Sorting Branch has somewhat relieved the congestion, there is already a demand for increased accommodation. The same thing has happened in Madras where there is a large Post and Telegraph Office facing the sea, designed by Mr. Chisholm and opened to the public in 1885. The expansion of business has outgrown the capacity of the building, and the time has come to construct a new post office and to use the present building as a Telegraph Office. Most head offices and important sub-offices are now designed to provide a proper hall for the public who wish to transact business, with a counter for clerks and sufficient open space in the building to allow each branch to work independently and in comfort under the supervision of a responsible officer. At Lahore, Nagpur, Patna, Chittagong, Bareilly, Rawalpindi, Cawnpore, Howrah, Poona, Agra, Allahabad, Mandalay, Benares, Sholapur and

Mount Road Madras, excellent offices have been recently constructed, and the next few years will see Rangoon, Delhi, Dacca, Darjeeling, Ajmere, Ahmedabad and several other large towns provided with post office buildings, not only scientifically planned, but handsomely designed.

Apart from its architectural features the essentials in a post office building are very much those of a bank, namely, space, facility for supervision and an arrangement of the branches dealing with the public, so that anyone entering the office to do postal business can find his way immediately to the clerk concerned. Space is most necessary, especially in the sorting and delivery of mails. In crowded offices thefts occur, packets of mails get mixed up and shot into wrong bags, and proper supervision is almost impossible. The old Indian system of letting the public stand in the veranda of the post office and transact business through the windows of the buildings has always been fatal to good and quick work. In the first place it is not easy to find the proper window for the exact purpose one requires, and there are seldom sufficient for all the branches. In the second place, when one has discovered the right window, the clerk is seated inside some distance away, and it is often difficult to attract his attention. The only sensible arrangement is a hall with a proper counter and screen on which the departments are clearly indicated, and the clerks sitting right up face to face with the public. The postal clerk has the gift of complete aloofness when his services are in the greatest request, but it requires extra strong nerves to feign indifference to a man who is looking straight at you two feet away and shouting his demands in unintelligible Hindustani, especially if he hasn't yet breakfasted and the weather is very hot. The real value of the counter is, in fine, that it enables all work with the public to be performed in half the time.

Except in the very largest offices where the postmaster sits in some secluded abode like an Olympian god, the postmaster's seat should be in the main office and readily accessible to the public. Deputy and assistant postmasters are very fine fellows, but nothing can compensate for the eagle eye of the Head. It is extraordinary how quickly a delivery gets out when he is present to urge it along, and how swiftly one gets one's money orders or savings bank deposits when he is looking on. For this reason he should be always within hail and, if he can accustom himself to deal courteously with the public and treat his staff with justice and consideration, he will be the man that the Post Office requires.

The policy in past years of obtaining rented buildings for post offices has proved a serious misfortune to the Department. They are seldom or never suitable for public offices, and the various attempts to adapt them for postal purposes have been expensive and unsuccessful. Every addition means an increase of rent and, with each renewal of the lease, the rental is regularly enhanced. I don't think that it is an exaggeration to say that throughout India the rents paid for Post Office buildings have increased by 50 per cent in the last twenty-five years. In many instances the total value of the house itself has been paid many times over, and the Department still continues to pay an exorbitant price for the privilege of occupying the ruins. No more miserable or extravagant policy than this can be imagined, and in large stations the Post Office is absolutely in the hands of the landlord who can demand what he likes when a lease

GENERAL POST OFFICE, BOMBAY

expires, a position which he is inclined to take full advantage of. In recent years the folly of this system has become more and more apparent, and efforts are now being made to provide Government buildings for all important offices, but any such scheme must necessarily take time since good sites in suitable positions are seldom available and funds are strictly limited.

A far-sighted man who thinks that his business will expand in time will provide for such expansion even as a speculation and, when expansion is a certainty as in the case of the Post Office which doubles its business in ten years, to provide merely for the needs of the moment is the falsest of false economy. The standard rule laid down by Sir Charles Stewart-Wilson with respect to new buildings was that, when a new post office is required, the space necessary for the office at the time should be taken and multiplied by two. Then there would be some hope of the accommodation being sufficient at all events for one official generation. There is hardly a single office built more than twenty years ago which is not now overcrowded and which will not have to be enlarged at considerable expense. If this lesson is taken to heart by the designers of our new post offices, they will earn the gratitude of future generations of postmasters.

CHAPTER XII

THE POST OFFICE IN INDIAN STATES

THE continent of India is divided into territory of two kinds, namely, British India and Indian States. There are 652 States with varying degrees of independence according to the treaties that exist between them and the British Government. Except in three of these, Mysore, Travancore and Cochin, no proper postal system can be said to have existed before the Imperial Post Office of India was established. In Mysore the Anche, a local post, was a very old institution, and its extension to the whole Kingdom was one of the earliest measures of the reign of Chikka Devaraj Wadayar in the year 1672. A similar system known as Anchel has existed for many years in Travancore and Cochin, but its origin is not known. Other States had no Post Offices in the proper sense of the term, and when the Post Office of India was established it extended its operations to many of these without any question. From many of the larger States, however, the Imperial Post Office was rigidly excluded, with the result that there was great difficulty in maintaining any postal communication between them and British India. Gradually certain States began to develop postal organizations of a distinct and independent character with special postage stamps of their own and others had organizations without any postage stamps. All kinds of different arrangements existed and the position is well described by Sir Frederic Hogg, the Director-General, in his Annual Report of 1878–9:

"In some places the delivery of correspondence proceeding from the Imperial Post is effected by an agency independent of this Department, in other places this agency is subject to Imperial Post control; while sometimes again both descriptions of distributing agencies are employed. There exists an arrangement under which the Imperial Post is subsidized for the delivery of correspondence, and there are some localities in Native territory which are destitute of any postal organization, and where letters cannot be delivered at all. Nor is diversity of method the sole difficulty that has to be met. Beyond the limits of this Department information on postal matters can hardly be obtained. Native States issue no *Postal Guide*, print no lists of post offices and publish no postal matters for the information of the public. Postal information is not available. It is uncertain whether a letter will ever be delivered. Not only is prepayment to destination in many cases impossible, but correspondence is subject on delivery to arbitrary and unknown charges. Registration is often impossible. Postcards don't exist and the inhabitants of Native States, which oppose Imperial Post extensions, are debarred from the benefits of the Money Order, Insurance and Value-Payable systems and other facilities afforded by the Imperial post office to the public. Restrictions of correspondence must be the natural consequence of this diversity of system or absence of system, and the only real remedy lies in the gradual extinction of all post organizations and their supersession by the Imperial Post. Such a measure must entail great expense for several years, but uniformity of postage rates, rules and conditions would result and the cost involved would doubtless ultimately be more than covered by increased revenue."

The first case that came prominently to notice was that of the Patiala State with which there was considerable trouble regarding postal exchanges. A proposal was made in 1880 to extend the Imperial Postal System to the State, but it was not acceptable to the Council of Regency, and after much discussion it was decided to prepare a Convention according to which a mutual exchange of correspondence could be arranged. The Convention was ratified in 1884 and similar ones were made with Gwalior, Jhind and Nabha in 1885 and with Faridkot and Chamba in 1886, the last four constituting with Patiala the group known as the Phulkian States. The Conventions with these States are all similar and to the following effect :—

(1) There shall be a mutual exchange of correspondence, parcels and money orders between the Imperial Post Office and the post offices of the Native State, this exchange including registered, insured and value-payable articles, and being governed by the rules of the *Indian Postal Guide*, as periodically published.

(2) Certain selected post offices in British India and in the Native States shall be constituted offices of exchange, and these offices shall be the sole media of exchange for insured and value-payable articles and money orders, and shall be entrusted with the duty of preparing the accounts arising from the exchange.

(3) Indian postage stamps and postal stationery overprinted with the name of the Native State shall be supplied by the Government of India on indent at cost price, and shall be used for the purpose of prepaying inland correspondence posted in the State.

(4) The Government of India shall bear the cost of conveying mails over British territory, and the Native State shall bear the cost of conveying mails within the limits of the State.

(5) The Imperial Post Office shall establish no new post offices in Native State territory without the permission of the Durbar, excepting at Railway Stations or within British Cantonments, the Durbar undertaking the establishment of any post offices or letter-boxes required in State territory by the Imperial Post Office.

(6) On foreign correspondence posted in the State, postage shall be prepaid only by means of Imperial postage stamps not bearing the overprint, postage stamps with such overprint not being recognized for the purpose.

(7) Monthly accounts shall be kept of the amounts due to the Imperial Post Office by the Native State and vice versa upon the money order exchange.

No sooner had these Conventions been agreed to than Government began to regret the step that had been taken, and it was then seen that real postal unity in the country could only be effected by the abolition of separate systems in the different States, a policy directly opposed to that which had been adopted towards

Gwalior and the Phulkian States. When, therefore, the Dewan or Prime Minister of Mysore asked for a Convention, he was met with a definite refusal, and an alternative proposal was made to the Mysore Government that the Imperial Post Office should undertake the postal service of the State. The proposal was accepted in 1887, and the Mysore Anche was abolished at the end of 1888. This measure of amalgamation, in which the Mysore Darbar rendered substantial assistance, was carried into effect from the beginning of 1889. The facilities afforded by the Indian Post Office, which were thus extended to the whole of Mysore, were fully appreciated by the people and resulted in a great development of postal business, the number of articles delivered having increased in the first year by no less than a million.

The case of Mysore was such a striking example of the benefits arising from the unification of a State Post Office with the Imperial system that Sir Arthur Fanshawe, the Director-General, used every endeavour to extend the policy to other States. The result was that the Kashmir State followed suit in 1894, and shortly afterwards Bamra, Nandgaon and Pudakottah. The efforts to win over Hyderabad, the premier State of India, were not successful. Although negotiations were extended over many years and every inducement was offered, the Nizam steadfastly refused to surrender the management of his own Posts as a separate system.

In 1906 Mr. Stewart-Wilson, who succeeded Sir Arthur Fanshawe as Director-General, started a fresh campaign for the unification of the Post Office all over India, and he succeeded in getting Indore and Bhopal to join in 1908. Since then Jaipur asked for a Conven-

GENERAL POST OFFICE, MADRAS

tion, but this was refused in accordance with the policy that Conventions were undesirable as only tending to perpetuate the many diversities which Government were anxious to abolish. The position at present is that out of 652 States, 637, including Faridkote which voluntarily abandoned its Convention in 1904, have cast in their lot with the Imperial Post Office. The number of outstanding States is thus fifteen, of which only Hyderabad, Gwalior, Jaipur, Patiala and Travancore are of much importance.

The policy of the Government of India has been clearly laid down in the correspondence dealing with the unification of the Hyderabad Posts with the Imperial Post Office. The Government is unwilling to take over the postal system of any State without the full consent of the Durbar or State Council, but it exercises the right of opening an Imperial post office or placing a letter-box anywhere in a State if Imperial interests require it. As a rule such offices are opened at railway stations or military cantonments, but they may be opened elsewhere in cases of real necessity. The aim of the Government is towards complete unification of the Post Office all over the country. The inconvenience of separate systems is keenly felt, and the inequality of Conventions on mutual terms between a great Empire and a small State is obvious. The principle upon which each country of the Postal Union retains its own postage on foreign correspondence is based on the theory that for every letter sent a letter is received, and that the transit charges are fairly apportioned, and in many cases the difference is slight when spread over a long period. When the principle is applied to a small State in a big country like India, the burden of handling correspondence is very unevenly divided. For every ten miles a letter has to be conveyed within the State, the Post Office of India may have to convey it a thousand miles or more at a cost altogether out of proportion to the postage receipts for half the correspondence handled. The difference is still more marked in the case of parcels and money orders and, despite all efforts to make the division of fees correspond with the work done by each administration, the position has never been satisfactory.

The postal future of the few States that still refuse to join the Imperial system is uncertain. All compromises have been rejected, and the arguments of prestige and prejudice are used to contest those of uniformity and convenience. As matters stand now the inconsistencies of small postal systems within the Indian Empire seem likely to continue until a firm hand on the one part and enlightened opinion on the other combine to abolish them.

CHAPTER XIII

THE OVERLAND ROUTE

OVERLAND trade between Europe and India has existed from the earliest times and was fully developed during the Roman Empire. After the overthrow of the Western Empire by Odoacer in A.D. 476 and during the struggles with the Persians and Saracens the overland trade with the East languished until the consolidation of the Saracenic power at Damascus, Cairo and Bagdad. It was again thrown into disorder by the ascendancy of the Turkish Guard at Bagdad, and did not revive until the thirteenth century, when, as the result of the Crusades, Venice and Genoa became the great emporia for Eastern spices, drugs and silks. The merchandise came by land to the ports of the Levant and the Black Sea, but the capture of Constantinople by the Ottoman Turks in 1483 drove the traffic to Alexandria, which continued to be the mart for Eastern wares until the discovery of the Cape route to India altered the whole conditions of trade.

The first historical attempt to reach England from India by the overland route was made in 1777 when Lord Pigot, Governor of Madras, was placed in confinement by his own Council. Both parties attempted to avoid loss of time in representing their case to the Board of Directors by despatching messengers up the Red Sea and across Egypt. The Council's messenger, Captain

Dibdin, managed to land at Tor near the mouth of the Gulf of Suez, to make his way across Egypt and finally to reach his destination. Not so Mr. Eyles Irwin, the messenger of the Governor. He sailed in the brig *Adventure*, and after many mishaps only succeeded in reaching Cosseir on the Red Sea in July, where he and his companions were detained by the Turks.

In 1778, after the fall of Pondicherry, Warren Hastings was determined that the good news should go home via Suez, and he engaged to send Mr. Greuber by a fast sailing packet to that port with the despatches. The proposal was strenuously opposed by Francis and Wheler, but Hastings, having Barwell on his side and a casting vote in Council, was able to carry out his intention. Mr. Greuber managed to get through by this route, but neither Hastings nor the Board of Directors anticipated the objections which the Ottoman Porte had to any navigation of the Red Sea by the Company's ships. In 1779 the Porte issued a firman putting a stop to all trade between Egypt and India by the way of Suez and decreed that ships from India could proceed only as far as Jeddah. If despatches were to be sent by Suez, the messenger conveying them had to travel from Jeddah by Turkish ship. This was a hopeless arrangement and meant endless delay, besides which the fate of messengers or of any Europeans crossing the desert between Suez and Cairo was very uncertain. The terrible dangers and difficulties of the journey are graphically described in Mrs. Fay's letters. Owing to the opposition of the Turkish Government the overland route was abandoned for some time, but in 1797 an arrangement was made with them and the company's cruiser *Panther*, under the command of Captain Speak, sailed in that year with despatches. She left Bombay on the 9th March and reached Suez on the 5th May, where she waited for three months for return despatches ; but since these did not arrive she returned to Bombay, and, being delayed by contrary winds at Mocha, finally arrived after an absence of thirteen months.

In 1798 the Government carried into execution a project which they had long been contemplating, namely, the establishment of a mail route from India to England by the Persian Gulf and Turkish Arabia. A number of packet boats were put on this service which plied between Bombay and Basrah once a month. Private correspondence was allowed to be sent by this route upon the following conditions:—

1. No letter was to exceed four inches in length, two in breadth, nor to be sealed with wax.
2. All letters were to be sent to the Secretary to Government with a note specifying the name of the writer and with the writer's name under the address, to be signed by the Secretary previous to deposit in the packet, as a warrant of permission.
3. Postage had to be paid upon the delivery of each letter at the rate of 10 rupees for a single letter weighing one-quarter of a rupee, for letters weighing half a rupee 15 rupees, and for letters weighing one rupee 20 rupees.

Two mails were sent by each despatch, one by Bagdad and one by Aleppo. We are not told if many private people were wealthy enough to pay these overwhelming rates of postage or were prepared to face the irksome conditions imposed upon anyone using this route.

In the first quarter of the nineteenth century the East

India Company continued to retain a Resident at Busra long after their trade had ceased to be of any consequence. One of his principal duties was in connection with the desert post, by which despatches were forwarded to England from the Bombay Government. Later on the post of Resident was abolished, and in 1833 the desert post was closed, as despatches, when forwarded overland, were sent in the Company's cruisers via Cosseir on the Red Sea and Cairo.

On the 5th November, 1823, a meeting was held in the Town Hall at Calcutta to discuss the feasibility of establishing communication with Great Britain by means of steam navigation via the Mediterranean, Isthmus of Suez and the Red Sea. A premium of £10,000 was offered to the first company or society that would bring out a steam vessel to India and establish the communication between India and England. The first steamer to reach India via the Cape was the *Enterprise*, commanded by Captain Johnson, in 1826. She was a vessel of five hundred tons burthen with two engines of sixty horse-power each and also built to sail, and she performed the journey in fifty-four days. Her great fault was want of room for coal, a circumstance which nearly led to a disaster on the voyage, as the coal, which had to be packed on top of the boilers, ignited and the fire was extinguished with difficulty. The credit for establishing the Suez route belongs to Lieutenant Thomas Waghorn, of the East India Company's Marine. He was the first to organize direct communication between England and India by means of fast steamers in the Mediterranean and Red Seas. In 1830 the steamer *Hugh Lindsay* made the first voyage from Bombay to Suez, and Waghorn from that time worked hard at his scheme. He built eight halting places in the desert between Cairo and Suez, provided carriages and placed small steamers on the Nile and the canal of Alexandria. Waghorn's triumph was on the 31st October, 1845, when he bore the mails from Bombay, only thirty days old, into London. This memorable feat settled the question of the superiority of the overland as compared with the old Cape route, but it was not given effect to without great opposition from the shipping companies.

In 1840 the Peninsular and Oriental Steamship Company obtained a charter of incorporation, and one of the conditions was that steam communication with India should be established within two years. This condition was fulfilled by the despatch of the *Hindustan* to India via the Cape of Good Hope in 1842. The advantages of the route across the isthmus of Suez were, however, too obvious, and the P. and O. Company took up a contract for the conveyance of mails between London and Suez, while vessels of the East India Company's navy conveyed them between Suez and Bombay. The journey from Alexandria to Suez was most uncomfortable for passengers. It was made by canal boat to Cairo, and then by two-wheeled vehicles across the desert to Suez. In 1844 a contract was given for five years to the P. and O. Company to establish a regular mail service in the Indian seas, with a subsidy of £160,000 a year for the combined India and China services. This contract was subsequently extended, and in January, 1853, a fresh contract was concluded with the Company under which fortnightly communication was secured between England, India and China, with a service once in two months between Singapore and Sydney. On the 7th July, 1854, a supplementary contract was entered into for the conveyance of mails between Southampton and Bombay through Alexandria, by which way the transit time was twenty-eight days. The total subsidy under both contracts was £224,300 a year. The sea postage collected by the United Kingdom and India was devoted to the payment of this subsidy, and any deficiency was borne equally by both countries. In 1867 a fresh contract for twelve years was concluded with the Company for a weekly service to and from Bombay and a fortnightly one to and from China and Japan. The annual subsidy was fixed at £400,000, to be increased to £500,000 if such should be necessary, in order to enable the Company to pay 6 per cent dividend upon their capital. This absurd clause was cancelled in 1870, and the annual subsidy was fixed at £450,000.

The Suez Canal was opened in 1869, but owing to difficulties with the British Government it was not used for the passage of the mail steamers until many years later. In 1880 the Southampton route was abolished, and the contract for the weekly service stipulated for a transit time of 17½ days between London and Bombay via Alexandria and Suez. It was not until 1888 that the mails were sent by the Suez Canal instead of by rail across Egypt.

During the term of the contract 1867–1869, the port for reception and despatch of mails was Marseilles. Arrangements were made in the new contract of 1869 for the substitution of Brindisi for Marseilles on the completion of the Mont Cenis Tunnel and railway, and Brindisi remained the European port for the reception and despatch of mails until the outbreak of war in 1914.

On the 1st July, 1898, a new contract was drawn up for a combined Eastern and Australian service. The transit time between London and Bombay was limited

POST OFFICE, AGRA

to 14½ days and the annual subsidy was fixed at £330,000, of which £245,000 represented the payment for the service between Brindisi, India, Ceylon, the Straits Settlements and China. The last contract was entered into with the Company on the 1st July, 1908, for seven years. The transit time between Brindisi and Bombay was reduced to 11½ days with an allowance of thirty-six hours in the monsoon, and the total subsidy was fixed at £305,000.

The present contract with the P. and O. Company expires in 1922, and what fate the future has in store for the Suez Canal route we cannot tell. There has been much talk of a through railway from Calais to Karachi, and with the Channel tunnel completed this would mean a railway route from London to India. The cost, however, of transporting the Indian mail, which often consists of more than ten thousand bags, over this enormous distance by rail would probably be prohibitive. Under the International Postal Convention each country traversed would have the right to claim a territorial transit charge, and with fast steamers between Marseilles and Bombay the saving in time might not be so great as has been anticipated.

Another competitor to the steamer service has appeared recently in the form of Aviation. Several proposals for an Air Mail Service between England and India have been made, but the success of long distance transits by air is not yet assured.

It has been stated that the old familiar scenes at Port Said and Aden will soon be as unknown to the Eastern traveller as Table Bay and St. Helena. The old trade routes are to be revived again, no longer with slow and picturesque caravans, but with rushing trains and aeroplanes. Despite these prophecies the P. and O. continue to build new ships, they book passages even a year ahead, and are preparing to tender for a new mail contract. Is this mere contempt, is it optimism, or is it the adoption of Warren Hastings' motto: "Mens aequa in arduis"?

CHAPTER XIV

THE SEA POST OFFICE

IN 1859 the Postmaster-General, United Kingdom, announced that it had been determined to open the homeward-bound mails on board the steamers between Alexandria and Southampton and Alexandria and Marseilles, with a view to effect a partial or complete sorting of the letters and newspapers. He also suggested that the clerks entertained for this service might during the voyage out be employed in sorting the letters and newspapers contained in the mails despatched from England to India. At the same time he inquired whether the Government of India would be willing to bear their proportion of the cost of the scheme. The offer was declined on the ground that English clerks could not sort letters correctly for stations in India, where there were many places with the same name.

In 1860 the Bombay Government reported that on the Europe side of Egypt the former practice of sending an Admiralty Agent with each steamer of the Peninsular and Oriental Company in charge of mails had been abolished, and instead the Company carried a couple of post office clerks to sort the homeward mail. They embarked on the Marseilles boat at Alexandria, and before arriving at Malta they sorted all the letters for transmission via Marseilles. At Malta these clerks were transferred to the vessel for Southampton, and when the steamer reached that port all the heavy mails were sorted. The Bombay Government suggested that a similar arrangement might be adopted east of Suez, the clerks told off for the work being employed in the Bombay post office when they were not engaged on the steamer. The Bombay Government's suggestion was negatived on the ground of expense in view of the unsatisfactory state of the Indian finances at the time.

In 1864 the subject was revived by Lord Lawrence. The Director-General, Mr. Monteath, agreed with the objections formerly urged that English Post Office clerks could not sort letters for all stations in India, but held that they could sort letters received by the Marseilles route only for Bombay and put up in boxes the letters and papers for the several Governments or Administrations in the provinces. It was then decided that sorting to the above limited extent might best be done in London and that, if it were done by a sorting establishment on a steamer west of Suez, the Indian Government might be reasonably called upon for a contribution. Thus the discussion ended for the time and nothing was done.

The subject was revived in 1868, when weekly communication between England and India was established. In the new contract with the Peninsular and Oriental Company provision was made to accommodate a postal sorting office and give free passages to sorters on the vessels east of Suez. The Government of India decided to take advantage of this arrangement and authorized experimental sea-sorting establishments on the scale of six sets of sorters for fifty-two voyages annually in each direction between Bombay and Suez. Each set consisted of a head sorter, a sorter and two packers. The calculation was based on an allowance of fifteen days each way for the voyage to and from Suez, with an interval of from two days to six days between a return from Suez and the next departure from Bombay. Notice was at the same time given for the withdrawal of the Naval Agents employed on board the steamers. One of the principal duties of these Naval Agents appears to have been to report whether penalties for delay should be exacted or not according to the circumstances in which the delays occurred.

In his final report in 1870 on the working of the system, as a result of which the establishment was permanently continued, the Director-General described the work of the sea post office as "embracing the sorting of mails for transmission to the various localities of a huge continent, as well as the checking of the accounts made out in respect of such correspondence by the various European offices from which the mails are received. . . . It is a work which, in an office on shore, would be distributed among a large establishment, each member of which would have to learn only a small portion of the business; and it is a work the bad performance of which even occasionally will give rise to the most serious consequences." The experimental formation of the sea-sorting office had succeeded so well that the inward overland mail was received at Bombay ready for despatch into the interior, instead of having to be detained there for about six hours, which often involved the loss of a whole day for certain places. The Bombay delivery ticket-holders got their overland letters at the post office window about ten minutes after the mail had arrived, and the delivery to Calcutta ticket-holders of letters, which had been sorted at sea, was similarly expedited.

The Indian sea-sorting office sorted letters for the United Kingdom, but the London General Post Office did not reciprocate by sorting the mail for India, the latter being done at sea, which enabled London to dispense with a large expenditure for Naval Agents. Although the revised contract with the Peninsular and Oriental Company provided for proper sorting accommodation on their vessels eastward of Suez, there was no similar provision westward of Suez; on the contrary, it was specially provided that the master or commander of the vessel should take charge of the mails to the west of Suez. The fact was that the work done by the Indian sea-sorting office on the homeward voyage was so complete and thorough that the British Post Office was able to abolish all its sea-sorting establishments west of Suez.

The steady growth in the work to be done and in the number of men required to cope with it gave rise to many difficulties in connection with the provision of suitable and adequate accommodation on board the steamers, the proper supervision of the staff, and the improvement of the service. The sorting arrangements had to be revised frequently, and the extent of the run, which, as stated above, was originally between Suez and Bombay, had in 1890 to be curtailed to the voyage between Aden and Bombay in consequence of the decision of the Peninsular and Oriental Company to tranship the outward and homeward mails at Aden every alternate week.

With the steady increase in the volume of the mails o be dealt with, it was found necessary to add to this staff considerably from time to time. In 1873 the total staff of the six sets comprising the "Marine Postal Service, Suez and Bombay," was raised to six mail officers, six assistant mail officers, six supernumerary assistant mail officers and twelve packers, i.e. five men for each set. When the journey was curtailed to the Bombay-Aden run the sets were reduced to three, but the number in each set had to be steadily increased until in 1908 it reached twenty-nine, consisting of an assistant mail officer, fifteen sorters and thirteen packers.

In the year 1899 a special inquiry, made in connection with a question asked in Parliament as to the effect of the introduction of Imperial penny postage on work in the sea post office, revealed the fact that the conditions of the service were very exacting on the staff. The extent to which the sorting of the mails could be done at Bombay or in the Railway Mail Service instead of at sea was very fully considered, and, although the Committee of postal officers convened at Bombay to examine the subject did not recommend the discontinuance of the existing arrangement, its retention was made conditional upon the adoption of a number of special measures to reduce the amount of work at sea.

A further inquiry into the conditions of service in the sea post office, instituted in the year 1905 in connection with a representation on the subject made to the Secretary of State for India by the late Mr. Samuel Smith, M.P., again brought into prominence the fact that the work had to be performed in circumstances of a peculiarly trying nature. It also established that, owing to the rapid increase, at the rate of 10 to 12 per cent a year, in the volume of the mails, the question of arranging for the sorting work to be done on shore instead of at sea could not be deferred much longer. This growth was bound to involve further additions to the staff from time to time, while the accommodation which it was possible to secure for the work, especially on board the through mail steamers, was strictly limited.

The subject of abolishing the sea post office altogether, or, at least, of restricting it to very small proportions, was again taken up in 1907, as the Postmaster-General, Bombay, reported that the service could not be placed on a proper footing without the provision of much more accommodation on board the through steamers, and expressed the opinion that the time had come for considering whether it was not possible to have most of the work of sorting done on shore.

By the end of 1908 the volume of the mails had become so large and the difficulty of dealing with them on board so great that a radical change was needed. The question of having the sorting work done on shore was, therefore, fully examined again with the Postmaster-General, Bombay. The position at the time was as follows: The mails for India despatched from the United Kingdom were received by the Aden-Bombay sea post office partly sorted for the various territorial divisions of India, and partly unsorted. The unsorted portion, which amounted to about 40 per cent of the total, consisted of the articles of all classes posted or received in London late on Friday evening, which the London General Post Office did not sort before despatch. The Indian mails from countries other than the United Kingdom were received by the sea post office wholly unsorted. With the exception of trade circulars and price lists, all the unsorted mails received were dealt with by the sea post office between Aden and Bombay. The average number of the unregistered letters, postcards, newspapers, packets of printed papers, and samples which had to be sorted by the sea post office on each voyage from Aden to Bombay was 150,000 and, in addition, some 7000 registered articles had to be specially treated and about 6000 unpaid articles examined and taxed with postage. This work had to be performed under very trying conditions and, during the monsoon season especially, the staff was hard pressed to finish the sorting before the steamer reached Bombay. The accommodation for sorting the mails provided on the through mail steamers was becoming less and less adequate as the volume of the mail increased and no additional space could be obtained.

The proposal to meet the situation by again extending the run of the sea post office to Port Said or Suez had to be negatived owing to the transhipment at Aden on alternate weeks. Moreover, it was undesirable to resort to a measure of this kind, as, quite apart from the large additional expenditure involved in return for insufficient advantages, the difficulty of keeping the staff under close and constant supervision was becoming more pronounced. In fact, this difficulty of exercising proper supervision over the enormous volume of work at sea furnished in itself a very strong argument in favour of having the work of sorting and dealing with these important mails done entirely on shore.

It was estimated that, with the provision of all necessary appliances and conveniences for dealing rapidly with the work on shore, a staff of about 150 well-trained and efficient sorters could do within a period of two and a half hours from the time of the *landing* of the mails the whole of the work then done by the sea post office. This number could be easily provided from among the sorters already employed in the sea post office, in the Bombay General Post Office, and in sections of the

Railway Mail Service working into and out of Bombay. The provision of suitable accommodation for the sorting to be done on shore, which was formerly a matter of much difficulty owing to the want of space in the General Post Office, Bombay, no longer existed as the new General Post Office near the Victoria Terminus, the building of which was then well advanced, had ample room for this purpose.

It was unnecessary to enter into any examination of the question in respect of the outward mails from India as the whole of the work done by the sea post office in connection with those mails could just as easily be performed, without any public or postal inconvenience and at very little extra cost, by the Railway Mail Service and in the various large post offices in India.

In view of the increasingly unfavourable conditions under which the sorting had to be performed at sea and of the greater security and efficiency that would be secured by having it done on shore, it was admitted that the best course would be to abolish the sea sorting service, but to do so gradually in order to avoid any dislocation in the disposal of the foreign mails. The various Indian Chambers of Commerce were consulted in 1911, and the general opinion was that no change should be made until the Alexandra Docks at Bombay were completed. The authorities of the Bombay Port Trust were accordingly requested to provide a sorting hall for the Post Office on the new pier. On the completion of the new mole in the harbour the mail steamer, instead of discharging its mails in the stream, would be able to berth alongside the pier ; the delay in transhipment would be greatly reduced, and with a sufficient staff of sorters on the spot the mails would be ready for despatch by the special trains due to leave Bombay within four and a half hours of the signalling of the steamers.

The question was finally settled by the outbreak of the War in 1914. The sailings of the mail steamers became very irregular, accommodation on board could no longer be provided for sorters, and consequently the sorting of both the outward and inward mails had to be performed in the Bombay General Post Office. The sorting of the homeward mail on shore was undertaken from the 15th August, 1914, and the last inward mail sorted on board arrived at Bombay on the 27th August, 1914. In spite of war conditions, the first special train usually started within seven hours of the steamer having been signalled. In these circumstances the sea post office was formally abolished as such, and the Indian share of the Eastern Mail Service subsidy was reduced by a sum of £8800 a year on account of its discontinuance.

No other Postal Administration of the world has ever attempted to undertake the task of sorting the foreign mails while in course of transit by sea on anything like the scale on which this work was done by the Indian Post Office. A certain amount of sorting of mails was done on the steamers of the White Star Line sailing between Liverpool and New York, and on those of the American Line sailing between Southampton and New York, also on board the German steamers sailing between Bremen or Hamburg and New York. The work done on those lines, however, was on a very minor scale and a small staff of four men on the White Star and American Line steamers, and of three on the German steamers was employed. The strength of the staff of the sea post office working between Bombay and Aden was, in 1914, one hundred and three men, divided into three sets of one assistant mail officer, seventeen sorters and fourteen packers each, with seven probationary sorters. The staff was a most extravagant one; the men were not employed for more than half their time. By using a large staff and with proper organisation the work that took five days at sea is now being done more efficiently in a less number of hours in Bombay.

Under present arrangements the mails are hoisted from the steamer direct into the Foreign Mail Sorting Office on the Ballard Pier. There they are opened and sorted for the various parts of India by about one hundred and fifty sorters, and within three hours they are ready for the postal special trains which leave the pier station for Calcutta, Madras, Lucknow and the Punjab. Foreign Mail Service sections work in each of these trains to deal with the final sorting and distribution of the mails to the various stations *en route*.

CHAPTER XV

THE POST OFFICE IN MESOPOTAMIA AND THE PERSIAN GULF

THE Great War has thrown such strong light on the countries which border on the Persian Gulf that it may be interesting to record the important part which has been played by the Post Office of India in connection with imperial policy in Persia and Mesopotamia.

Owing to political considerations and the necessity of keeping open alternative means of communication between Europe and India, the importance of the Persian Gulf and Mesopotamia as a mail route was established nearly a century and a half ago. The ships of the old Indian Navy carried mail packets from Bombay to Basra, which was the starting-point of a regular dromedary post to Aleppo, linked with a horse post from Aleppo to Constantinople, and it is an interesting piece of history that Lord Nelson's letter to the Bombay Government, giving the news of the naval victory of the Nile, was transmitted by this route.

During the first half of the last century, as the Persian Gulf and the Shat-el-Arab were infested with pirates, these waters were avoided by British trading vessels, so that, when a ship of the Indian Navy was not available to convey mails to Bombay, letters from the Political Residents of the East India Company stationed at Bagdad and Basra were sent to India by the desert route via Damascus and Beyrout and thence through Egypt, and correspondence between Bushire and India had to be diverted through Teheran and Alexandria. In 1862 a regular six-weekly mail service between Bombay and Basra was undertaken by the British India Steam Navigation Company, and about the same time the Euphrates and Tigris Steam Navigation Company agreed to extend the mail service from Basra to Bagdad by running their steamers in connection with the ocean line. The postal system at the coast ports, however, was defective owing to the absence of local post offices for the collection and distribution of mails, but these were gradually established from the year 1864 onwards at Bushire, Muscat, Bandar Abas, Bahrain, Mohammerah, and other places under the protection of British Consular officers, and post offices were opened at Bagdad and Basra in Turkish Arabia in 1868.

Although all these post offices were primarily intended for the benefit of political officers of the Government of India, they have proved just as useful to the consular representatives of other European nations and to the public, and there is no doubt that, by supplying a commercial want, they gave a great impetus to trade in the Persian Gulf region. For years there was no other local postal service worthy of the name, and intercourse with the hinterland was entirely under the control of the British Consular officers. In 1868 Turkish Arabia was wholly dependent for regular communication with the outside world on English enterprise. There were two mail routes from Bagdad, one to Teheran via Kermanshah, a distance of 480 miles, and the other from Bagdad to Damascus, 500 miles, in connection with the British Consulate at the latter place and the route to

England via Beyrout. A monthly mail service was also maintained by the Government of India for the convenience of the British Legation at Teheran and the Residency of Bushire, the route lying through Shiraz and Ispahan, where British agencies had been established, but no postage was charged on letters despatched, as the line was kept up purely for political purposes. In addition to this post the Indo-European Telegraph Department had a weekly service from Bushire to Shiraz. These Persian lines were worked partly by runners and partly by horsemen, and continued until the Persian Government inaugurated its own service in 1877 and established a weekly post between Bushire and Teheran.

The Turkish representative at the International Postal Congress held at Berne in 1878 urged that all foreign post offices in the Ottoman dominions should be suppressed, but the demand was rejected as it involved a diplomatic question outside the province of the Congress. In 1881 the Turkish Government established a dromedary post between Bagdad and Damascus in opposition to the English consular overland post and, after repeated representations on the part of the Ottoman Government, the latter was abolished in 1886 after having been in existence for upwards of a hundred years. In the following year the Ottoman Government closed their own line, and the only direct route left open to Europe was the Turkish post via Mosul on the Tigris to Constantinople. When reporting the closing of the British desert post, the British Consul-General at Bagdad asked the Postmaster-General in London to warn the British public not to post anything of value by any route other than the one from London to

Bombay and thence by sea to Basra and Bagdad, and the numerous complaints of the loss of parcels, books and letters fully justified his want of confidence in the Ottoman post.

The British post offices at Basra and Bagdad and the service by river steamer between these two ports were subjected to marked hostility on the part of the Turks, notwithstanding the continued efforts of the British Consular officer to limit their functions. Competition with the local Ottoman postal institutions was never aimed at, and Indian post offices were primarily and chiefly maintained for Consular purposes and located in the Consulate buildings. Local traders, however, were not slow to discover the advantage of the safe transit offered by the Indian mail service and the convenience of the parcel post system, but their efforts to avoid payment of Customs dues on articles imported by this means were frustrated at the outset by the British Consul-General of Bagdad, Sir Arnold Kemball, who went so far as to suspend the parcel traffic in the interests of the Turkish Government until the latter could make adequate provision for Custom-House examination and levying of dues on both import and export parcels. After various methods of detecting and dealing with dutiable parcels had been tried for many years, the system of handing over all inward parcels received from the offices of exchange at Bombay, Karachi and Bushire to the Turkish Customs at Bagdad and Basra with copies of the Customs declarations and invoices received was adopted by the Consular post offices, the addressees being required to take delivery at the Customs House on presentation of a delivery order signed by the British-Indian postmaster.

Anyone who has had experience of the vagaries of Turkish Customs House officials can sympathize with people whose goods fell into their hands. The smallest irregularity, however unintentional, detected in a declaration or manifest could only be set right by the liberal distribution of bribes. Woe betide the scrupulous owner or consignee who declined to adopt such methods and decided instead to stand by his rights and carry his complaint to higher authorities. The story is told of a young missionary lady whose wedding outfit was packed into a box which was taken in custody by a Turkish official and was detained for the ostensible purpose of examination of the contents and assessment of duty. The settlement of this knotty point proceeded in a leisurely fashion for weeks, because the owner's conscience or purse would not permit of her speedily clinching the matter by a suitable payment. When the box was finally delivered the addressee found, to her horror, that the wedding dress and other articles of her trousseau bore unmistakable traces of having been worn. To add insult to injury, the Customs authorities threatened to confiscate the goods, saying that there was a prohibition against the importation of "worn clothes"! There is no doubt that they had been freely used by the harem of some Ottoman Customs official, as the curiosity of Turkish ladies regarding the latest European fashions was notorious and could usually overcome official scruples.

When the Inland Insurance system was introduced in India in 1877 it was extended to the post offices in the Persian Gulf and Turkish Arabia. The Insured Parcel Post was used largely by traders at Bagdad, Basra and Bushire for the exportation of specie, and the total value insured in 1882–83 amounted to over twenty-four lakhs of rupees. The pearl merchants at Bahrain, which is the centre of the pearl fisheries in the Gulf, availed themselves largely of the Insured Parcels Post for the export of valuable parcels of pearls. Protests were soon lodged by the British India Steam Navigation Company, which held the mail contract, against this competition on the part of the Post Office on the ground that it infringed their monopoly. They argued that the carriage of specie and pearls was almost the sole source of profit from the Persian Gulf service, and after a careful review of the whole question it was decided in 1885 to abolish insurance of parcels and letters to and from the British post offices in the Gulf and Turkish Arabia. This measure resulted in a heavy loss in postal revenue, but was only fair to a Company which had risked much in maintaining British trade relations with that part of the world, and which has done more than any other to throttle German competition.

The steamship companies employed to carry mails have all along had to contend with serious difficulties at the Gulf ports. The original mail service undertaken by the British India Steam Navigation Company between Bombay and Basra, and by the Euphrates and Tigris Steam Navigation Company between Basra and Bagdad, was a six-weekly one, but a monthly service was arranged in 1866 and a fortnightly service in 1870. From 1878 onwards mails were despatched weekly in both directions, and this has been supplemented in recent years by a fast service in connection with the English mail, the steamers calling only at the principal intermediate ports. There were many obstacles to speedy transit and delivery of mails, such as absence of lights and buoys, want of harbour facilities at the Persian ports, difficulties of navigation in the river Tigris during the dry season, obstruction on the part of the authorities, especially the Turks, and difficulty of obtaining regular labour at the various anchorages. At many places the mail steamers have to anchor far out in the roadstead, and in rough weather there is some risk and delay in landing and embarking mails. The mail contract with the British India Steam Navigation Company required that mails should be exchanged during daylight, and three hours were specified for the purpose ; but this condition could not always be observed, and it was in the power of the local postmaster to upset all arrangements. Unrest was a common feature of the political life of these parts, especially when there was a change of Governors, and the authorities were generally too feeble to cope with a rising among the Arab or Persian tribes without the assistance of British bluejackets or Indian troops, who were not always available on the spot. At such times the Indian postmaster used to shut up his office long before darkness set in and barricade himself and his mails in the inner rooms of the building, so that the ship's mail officer arriving at dusk had no easy task in getting access to him. On one occasion the Political Resident of the Persian Gulf, whose word is law in these regions, was a passenger by the mail steamer which arrived at a certain port on a very sultry summer evening. Being anxious that the steamer should sail to Karachi without unnecessary delay, he asked the captain to expedite its departure, and the latter, who had previous experience of the local post office, said that he had his doubts about receiving the mails before morning, but promised to try his best, and went ashore himself. Two hours later a message came to the ship asking for the Political Resident's personal assistance, and there was nothing left for the distinguished official to do but to go to the office himself. He found the captain and his second officer pelting the roof of the post office with stones, while from inside issued forth the vilest abuse of all ships' captains and their relations, with threats to report the attack to the Resident. The matter was eventually settled, and the story is still told by all the natives with great gusto, as the Eastern mind sees a special humour in the setting down of an important official.

The Euphrates and Tigris Steam Navigation Company, owned by Messrs. Lynch Brothers, during the many years of its existence was never able to obtain permission from the Ottoman Government to run more than two steamers between Basra and Bagdad. The distance is five hundred miles, and, as the paddle-boats had occasionally to tie up during the night when the river was low, it is not surprising that the weekly mail service each way had no reputation for regularity. There were several other causes which contributed to misconnection between these boats and the ocean-going mail steamers of the British India Company. The run from Basra to Bagdad and vice versa was usually accomplished in five days, which left only two days at either end for loading and unloading, cleaning and repairs of engines and other duties. If a steamer reached port towards the end of the week, little or no work could be done. Friday is a general holiday among the Turks and Arabs who are Mohammedans, and the Customs House is kept closed; Saturday is the Hebrew Sabbath, when Jews are absent from the wharves; while Sunday is a *dies non* with the Armenian Christians, who are among the most important of the shippers. It was hard for an European merchant to contend with such an accumulation of sacred days. He was willing to keep open and work on every day of the week, but the susceptibilities of the local population cannot be overridden. The Turkish Government tried every conceivable method of hindering the enterprise of Messrs. Lynch and Company, but their steamers continued to flourish and gain in popularity, whereas the Ottoman line of steamers, established in 1867 under the auspices of the Government with the avowed object of smashing the British line, failed to justify its existence. The Turkish steamers were badly equipped and inefficiently controlled, and being always in a state of dilapidation became a byword of reproach even among the Turkish subjects of Mesopotamia. It was not surprising, therefore, that overtures on the part of this Company to obtain the English contract for the carriage of mails were never seriously considered. Apart from the unreliability of the service, there were strong political grounds for supporting the Company which had done so much under the British flag to open up the commerce of Mesopotamia.

Originally the merchants at the intermediate river ports of Kurnah, Kut and Amara, on the Tigris, were accustomed to post letters on the river mail boats and the clerk on board acted as a sort of travelling postmaster, but it was not long before the Turkish authorities raised objections to this practice as an infringement of their postal rights, notwithstanding that they had a concession of free carriage of Turkish official correspondence through the British Post. After much correspondence and discussion between the Indian Political and Postal authorities it was decided not to allow the mail steamer to be used as a post office. Consequently all letters posted on board were made over to the Ottoman post offices, and this procedure was also followed in respect of local postings in the British post offices at Basra and Bagdad for all places in Turkish Arabia.

The purely Consular status of the Post Office in the Persian Gulf region was shown by the fact that our mail bags for Bagdad were always labelled "H.M.'s Consul-General, Bagdad," and those for Basra directed to "H.M.'s Consul," special seals with the Royal Arms being used. The British Indian postmasters at these places held no written communication with Turkish officials, and the rule was that all such correspondence should pass through the Consul or Consul-General. Service privileged correspondence between Turkish Government departments, if properly franked, was allowed to pass free of postage through our post offices at Bagdad and Basra, and registered letters or packets suspected to contain precious stones, jewellery and other valuables liable to duty were transferred to the local Customs House.

The Indian Post Office in Mesopotamia and the Persian Gulf was not only the handmaiden of British commercial enterprise for many years, but also helped in an unostentatious way to consolidate our position and influence in those regions. Over thirty years ago a Persian Gulf division was formed under the control of an European Superintendent who had to supervise and visit the offices regularly. The postmasters are either Indian Christians, Mohammedans or Hindus, and they are invested by the backward and unenlightened inhabitants of the remote Gulf ports with mysterious powers as the representatives of the great Indian Government. Wild-looking Central Asian traders armed with dagger and pistol, who bring down camel-loads of carpets, dried fruit and other merchandise from the interior of Persia and the Mekran; courtly and picturesque Arab horse-dealers who ship their thoroughbreds to Bombay every year; sleek Persians in their sky-blue tunics; emancipated negro slaves—all trust the postmaster in matters relating to their private business as they would never trust one of their own kind. The arrival of the weekly mail at a Persian Gulf port is like a festival. The precincts of the post office are thronged with a large and motley crowd drawn from all grades of the populace. Letters are delivered on the premises on this day, and everyone who has any link with the outer world is present on the off-chance of getting a communication through the post. The postmaster or his munshi stands at an open window calling out the addresses on the letters, the owners holding up their hands when they hear their names called. Most letters are prefixed with the word "Haji," which denotes that the recipients are good Mohammedans who have made the pilgrimage to the Prophet's tomb at Mecca. The deep, guttural Arabic or the soft Persian response is occasionally broken by a reply in the more familiar Hindustani or Gujrati, for in each Gulf port there is a small colony of Hindu traders from the West coast of India, easily distinguishable by their alert and business-like appearance. Women are conspicuous by their absence—more so, in fact, than in other Eastern countries—but, after the crowd has dispersed, a closely veiled and sheeted figure occasionally glides to the window and in plaintive tones asks for some service, the performance of which she must personally see to in the absence of her lord and master from home.

The Great War completely altered the conditions in Mesopotamia. In consequence of the Turkish Government having ordered the closure of all foreign post offices within their territory, the Indian post offices at Bagdad and Basra were closed under protest on the 1st October, 1914. The sub-postmaster, Basra, continued at work settling the affairs of his office until the 27th October, 1914, and left for India next day, whereas the Postmaster, Bagdad, was made a prisoner on the outbreak of hostilities with Turkey on the 1st November, 1914, and the post office property in his charge fell into the hands of the Turks.

The formal entry into Basra by British troops was made on the 23rd November, 1914, and the postal service was undertaken by the Indian Field Post Office. The service was developed and extended as the troops advanced. A railway was constructed from Basra to Amara and from Kut-el-Amara to Bagdad, and a regular mail service has been introduced by river steamers between Amara and Kut-el-Amara. The transit time of mails between Basra and Bagdad has thus been reduced to two days. Excellent jetties have now been built at Basra, so that much time is saved in loading and unloading mails, and, with well-equipped post offices at all important places, the postal service of Mesopotamia has become quite efficient.

Since the Armistice in 1918 the Indian Field Post Offices have been gradually withdrawn and have been replaced by civil offices under a Civil Director of Postal Services. The occupied territory in Mesopotamia is known as Iraq, and Turkish postage stamps overprinted with the words "Iraq under British Occupation" were introduced in 1918. On the 1st May, 1919, the Military Director of Postal Services was withdrawn and the postal administration of the country handed over to the Civil Director, who is now an official of the Local Government. A few Indian field post offices are still retained for the troops stationed beyond the frontiers of Iraq, but these will be closed as soon as military operations are finished.

The first Civil Director of the Post Office of Iraq was Mr. C. J. E. Clerici, an officer of the Indian Establishment. Almost the whole staff consists of men from the Post Office of India, and will continue to do so until local men have been trained in postal work. Indian inland postage rates were at first charged for correspondence exchanged between India and Iraq, but from the 1st September, 1919, the British Imperial foreign rates of postage were introduced. With the exception of four post offices on the Persian Gulf—namely, Koweit, Abadan, Mohammerah and Ahwaz, which are being administered by Iraq—the other Indian post offices in the Persian Gulf area are still under the control of the Post Office of India.

Such is the history of the establishment of the Indian Post Office in Mesopotamia and the Persian Gulf region. It began with the opening of small offices for the British Consular Agencies and commercial establishments of the East India Company. The public, however, were not slow to take advantage of the means of communication thus provided, and, despite the strenuous opposition of the Ottoman Empire, a really efficient postal system was organized. The extension of the Bagdad Railway, the Euphrates Valley irrigation project and the opening of the Anglo-Persian oil field, whose pipe-line terminates on the Shat-el-Arab, are the three great factors in the development of Mesopotamia. This country already occupies a prominent place in the affairs of the Empire, and, situated, as it is, on a main highway between East and West, it is possible that the region, which was the centre and cradle of the earliest civilization of the world, will recover its old importance. When this has been achieved the Post Office of India will always be able to look back with pride on the pioneer work which it has done in its quiet, unassuming way during the past half century.

CHAPTER XVI

THE POST OFFICE DURING THE INDIAN MUTINY

EVERY student of the history of the Indian Mutiny of 1857 knows the part played by the Indian Telegraph Department during that great crisis. The famous telegram of warning which was transmitted to the principal stations in the Punjab by two young signallers of the Delhi office (Messrs. Brendish and Pilkington) upon their own initiative on the morning of the 11th May, 1857, when the Meerut rebels, flushed with success, crossed the bridge of boats over the Jumna and entered the city of Delhi to join hands with their comrades there, is a splendid example of an assumption of responsibility followed by prompt action. Sir Herbert Edwardes refers to the final telegraphic message sent by Brendish to Mr. Montgomery, the Judicial Commissioner at Lahore, in these terms:

" When the mutineers came over from Meerut and were cutting the throats of the Europeans in every part of the Cantonment, a boy, employed in the telegraph office at Delhi, had the presence of mind to send off a message to Lahore to Mr. Montgomery, the Judicial Commissioner, to tell him that the mutineers had arrived and had killed this civilian and that officer, and wound up his message with the significant words ' we're off.' That was the end of the message. Just look at the courage and sense of duty which made that little boy, with shots and cannon all round him, manipulate that message, which, I do not hesitate to say, was the means of the salvation of the Punjab."

In the General Report of the Telegraph Department for the year 1857–58 the Director-General remarked:

"The value of that last service of the Delhi office is best described in the words of Montgomery: 'The electric telegraph has saved India.'"

Excellent work was also done by Post Office officials during the Indian Mutiny, but unfortunately it is forgotten owing to its having received little historical recognition. A perusal of musty records which lie in the archives of the Indian Government reveals a record of duties well performed in the midst of insuperable difficulties and dangers of which the Department may well be proud.

At the time of the Mutiny the British Army in India was deficient in the organization of two branches indispensable to the success of military operations in the field, and it was left to the Post Office to supply the want to a considerable extent. The Intelligence and Transport Departments were in their infancy, and the military authorities were not slow to take advantage of facilities afforded by the Post Office. At the commencement of the outbreak it was evident that postmasters in the affected districts were in a position to keep the authorities accurately informed of the direction in which the rebellion was spreading and to report the movements of the mutineers as long as the postal lines of communication remained intact, especially in the districts where there

GROUP OF SENIOR OFFICERS IN 1907

P. ROGERS H. A. SAMS C. H. HARRISON C. H. HOGG E. R. JARDINE G. R. CLARKE

R. A. DORAN H. S. HUTCHINSON C. STEWART WILSON H. C. SHERIDAN W. MAXWELL

Director General

were no telegraph lines or where the wires had been cut. Many officials—European, Eurasian and Indian—were killed at the outset, post offices being looted and destroyed and mails intercepted on the various lines wherever the rebels were in power. Much valuable information regarding such occurrences was collected and passed on to the authorities by postal employés in remote places. For transport, the Army had ready at hand, on the trunk roads of India, the machinery of the Post Office horse transit and bullock train, which was then in a high state of efficiency, and was able to render incalculable service in connection with the forward movement of troops and munitions of war as well as the despatch down country of wounded officers and men—and of refugees when the campaign was well advanced. After the final Relief of Lucknow by Sir Colin Campbell many of the ladies and children of the garrison were conveyed by this means in safety to Calcutta.

The Sepoy Mutiny began at Meerut on the 10th May, 1857. From the 18th May, 1857, onwards telegrams and letters were received at the Director-General's headquarters in Calcutta from the postmasters at Allahabad, Benares, Umballa and other stations, reporting the stoppage of mail communication with places which had fallen into the hands of the mutineers. News was also thus given of the destruction of post offices and plunder of mails at Sitapore, Indore, Hirapore, Cawnpore, Shahazadpore, Daryabad, Saugor, Segombe, Hamirpur, Jaunpor, Azimgarh and many more places. On the 15th May, 1857, the Postmaster-General, North-Western Provinces, gave instructions to his postmasters to collect waggons and bullocks for the conveyance of troops. On the 21st May the Postmaster, Agra, reported to the Director-

General that Dr. Clark, who had been specially vested with the authority of Postmaster-General in a portion of the North-Western Provinces, was safe and well at Muttra, and was trying to open mail communication. On the 26th May, 1857, the Postmaster, Benares, applied to the Director-General for authority to supply horses for conveyance of troops. Mr. H. B. Riddell, Director-General at the time, was fully alive to the situation and set a brilliant example to all ranks. He addressed the following letter to the Government of India from his camp at Sherghotty on the 30th May, 1857 :—

"I have the honour to report that arrangements have been made or are in train which will, I trust, enable the Bullock Train establishment to convey daily without interruption one hundred men from Raneegunge to Benares. There will be fifty-six pairs of Bullocks at each stage between Sherghotty and Benares.

"The Bullocks procurable are of the smallest and most miserable description. . . .
A workshop will be established at Dehree and, as the road over the sand of the Soane will be broken up in a day or two, the men of each detachment will be conveyed over in country carts, fresh waggons being ready on the other side. I shall probably have to stay to-morrow and make some arrangements at the Soane, but will, after doing so, move on to Benares and arrange for the despatch of troops from Benares to Allahabad. If the Commissariat bullocks are stationed along the line and they have any covered carts, large detachments can be sent every two or three days, but I will telegraph what can be done when I reach Benares. In the meantime Commissariat Gun bullocks should be stationed along the line."

The Director-General's efforts were ably seconded by Mr. C. K. Dove, Postmaster-General, and Mr. Garrett, Deputy Postmaster-General of Bengal, both of whom did all in their power to ensure the prompt despatch of troops up country, calling in the aid of the local magistrates to secure the best cattle and the services of the Engineering Department to facilitate the passage of carts over unbridged rivers along the Grand Trunk Road.

On the 2nd July, 1857, it was arranged to place the whole of the Bullock Train establishment north of Benares at the disposal of the military authorities. The transfer was made at the instance of General Havelock, who had just assumed command of the troops at Allahabad. He decided to use the Bullock Train entirely for the transport of stores and ammunition to the front and, when the rains had broken and the rivers became navigable, to convey troops by river steamers, a far more convenient and expeditious means than road conveyance. When it was necessary to use the roads, elephants were provided by the Commissary-General at Calcutta and by local zemindars (landholders).

On the 29th July, 1857, the Government of India published a notification authorizing the Chief Covenanted Civil or Military officer at every station throughout India where there was a post office under a Deputy Postmaster and no resident Postmaster had been specially appointed, to assume the office of Postmaster or to assign the office to some other Covenanted Civil or Military Officer at the station, reporting the arrangement in each instance for the information of the Postmaster-General of the Presidency. The Deputy Postmaster was to perform duties connected with the post office under the orders of the Postmaster so appointed. The functions of Inspecting Postmasters remained unaffected by this order, and post offices at places where there was no covenanted Civil or Military Officer were left in charge of the Deputy Postmasters. These orders were necessitated by the interruption of mail communication between many post offices and their head-quarters and the difficulty of control being exercised by Postmasters-General who were not always in a position to issue prompt instructions to their subordinates in matters of importance or emergency. At the same time no general power of censorship over correspondence was granted to officers, nor was anything done to diminish public confidence in the Government mail service.

Reports regarding the plunder of mails continued to come in from places as far removed as Kolhapur in the Southern Mahratta country and Bahraich in the United Provinces. Mails between Bengal and the United Provinces on one side and the Punjab on the other had to be diverted via Bombay, the Commissioner of Sind taking the responsibility for their safe despatch through Hyderabad (Sind). Many of the reports from post-masters referred to fresh outbreaks, and the movements of mutineers who did not hesitate to remove dak horses from relay stations on the mail routes whenever they had the chance. The information contained in these letters was duly passed on to the military authorities.

In connection with the correspondence for the army in the field, post offices were organized to accompany the movable columns under General Havelock, the Malwa Field Force and later the divisions commanded by General Outram and other distinguished leaders. During the campaign soldiers' letters were exempt from forward postage.

The large tract of country known as the North-Western Provinces and Oudh was the focus of the disturbance of 1857, and the strain put upon the postal officials in those provinces was greater than in other affected parts of the country. Most of the post offices and mail lines had to be closed at the beginning of the outbreak and were reopened one by one, as order was gradually restored by the British forces. A most interesting narrative of the interruption in the mail arrangements in the North-Western Provinces and Punjab subsequent to the outbreak at Meerut and Delhi on the 10th and 11th May, 1857, was supplied by Mr. Paton, Postmaster-General, and will be found in Appendix G.

As might be expected, the outbreak of the Mutiny caused a complete disorganization of postal communications, and the task of restoring mail lines in hostile territory was no easy one. The pay offered by the Department was not sufficient to induce men to risk their lives in isolated places, which were always open to attacks by the mutineers or by bands of armed villagers, and it is characteristic of the Indian Government at the time that they expected men to serve for salaries which were admitted to be inadequate even in times of peace. I will quote extracts from the reports of the Postmasters-General of the North-Western Provinces, Bengal and Bombay, which throw an interesting light upon the difficulties with which the Post Office had to contend in these troublous times.

Report of the Postmaster-General, North-Western Provinces, for the year ending the 31st March, 1858:

" In consequence of the rebellion, the Post Offices and lines of postal communication in the North-Western Provinces and Oudh were closed more or less, nearly throughout the year under review, and many of those in Oude and Bundelkund have not yet been reopened, owing to a portion of the above Provinces being still in the hands of the rebels, so that a report of the transactions of the present year is chiefly a narrative of the effects of the disturbances on the Post Office Department. The results shown herein cannot therefore be fairly compared with those of the previous years.

"The number of complaints of the loss and missending of letters during the year under review is comparatively greater than many of the previous years, which is chiefly owing to the frequent loss of the mails on different lines of road by rebels, their transmission by circuitous routes from the direct lines being closed or unsafe, and their irregular despatch by inexperienced hands employed in the Camp Post Offices.

"The proportion of bearing to paid or stamped letters is 0.974 to 1, which shows a progressive increase in the number of the former. This may be fairly attributed to the general habit of the natives, especially those in the army, and also among lower classes to despatch their letters bearing, more particularly at this period, when, from the constant movements of the troops from one place to another and the disturbed state of the country, they are undoubtedly liable to miscarry.

"I may also observe that a very large number of letters posted by the military and lower classes of the people are intended for places in the interior of districts, and, as the District Post establishments have not yet been fully reorganized, there is no guarantee for their punctual or safe delivery. Natives, being real economists, naturally prefer the despatch of their letters bearing, and so prevent any loss from prepayment of postage.

"The staff of the Department was much reduced by casualties during the late mutinies, and much difficulty has been experienced in procuring properly qualified persons to accept employment. A large number of offices having had to be hastily reopened, the demand for English-speaking clerks has been unprecedented, and, without raising the salaries, I could not fill up the vacancies in the Post Office.

"It is not a matter of surprise that extraordinary difficulty has been experienced in reorganizing the Post Office in such a crisis, when it is recollected that the salaries allowed to the officers of the Department are on a scale below that generally obtained in other Departments, that there are no holidays allowed them, and that leave of absence, excepting on medical certificate, is in a measure prohibited, owing to the establishment being generally on such a minimum scale as not to admit of any one being absent without providing a trained substitute.

"But notwithstanding an increase to the salaries of the officials having been generally granted to the extent that I have represented as necessary, I regret to have to record that I have not yet been able to complete the revision of all the office establishments to my satisfaction. There are still many incompetent officials in the Department, whom I am obliged to tolerate, until I meet with better qualified persons to take their places.

"As might be expected from an inexperienced or untrained establishment, working under great disadvantages, a comparatively large number of complaints of the missending and loss of letters have been received during the year under review, and, though every care has been taken to prevent mistakes, yet, from the circumstance of the direction on letters being often hastily and illegibly written, and the army, in numerous detached parties, constantly in the field, without their locality or destination being correctly known to the Post Office, the percentage of missent covers for the troops has unavoidably been great.

"I have again to remark the increase in the number of bearing letters; but considering the unsettled state of these Provinces, it is only what might be expected. I need not here repeat the reasons which induce the non-commercial class of natives to send their letters bearing postage.

"Taking into consideration the variety of languages in which native letters are generally written, and the very careless and illegible manner in which the directions and the names of addressees and senders are given, I am of opinion that the proportion disposed of at my office (being about 33 per cent on the whole number received) is satisfactory."

Report of the Postmaster-General, Bengal, for the year 1857–58:

"The mutinies which broke out in the North-Western Provinces in May, 1857, were also felt during the past year in the Bengal Presidency, and parts of the province were more or less affected by them, but, happily for Bengal, the interruptions and disorganization to her Postal Department caused by them were, by the adoption of prompt and vigorous measures, speedily restored. The Post Office Department, however, did not escape—a Deputy Postmaster and an Overseer were killed, a runner was wounded, a number of post offices, especially in Behar, were plundered, and a number of mails and mail packets were seized and destroyed by the mutinous sepoys.

"The rebellion of Koer Sing and the mutinies of the Dinapore sepoys interrupted and closed for a short time a portion of the Grand Trunk Road between Saseram and Benares, and the insurgents carried off some cattle belonging to the Department, and also burnt down some dak bungalows above Sherghotty.

"The revolt of the hill tribes on the southern line in the neighbourhood of Sumbulpore disturbed the communication with Bombay via Sumbulpore, which had been opened after the interruption of communication with Bombay by the Jubbulpore road, and the rebellion of the Ramghur Battalion disorganized the daks for a while in the South-West Frontier Agency between Chota Nagpore and Chyebassa.

"The mutinies of the Chittagong sepoys and the Segowlee insurgents caused only the destruction of some packets that fell into their hands, but passed off without any serious interruption to any mail line in Bengal."

Report of the Postmaster-General, Bombay, for the year 1857–58:

"The mutinies imperilled and interrupted almost every line in the Presidency; the foot lines were obliged to be strengthened, diverted, abandoned and reopened as circumstances required; those most severely tried were in Malwa, Rajpootana, Khandeish, Berar, the Southern Mahratta country and Guzerat, on some of which double pay and double numbers were scarcely sufficient to keep them open, and it was only by the activity, local knowledge, morale and reliance of the inspecting officers (always supported strongly by the Civil officers), whose powers were discretionally enlarged by me, that the lines were sustained.

"It is remarkable that in the midst of universal disturbance (especially in Malwa and Rajpootana), when distrust and confusion were at their height, and opportunities for plunder were frequent, and detection next to impossible, only one case occurred, or rather was brought home, in which the carriers of the mails either personally plundered or wilfully destroyed them.

"Although animosity was directed against the servants of the Post Office in common with every class of persons in Government employ, it was not especially so in this Presidency against the Post Office, unless where the collections offered temptation, as at Indore, Erinpoora, Neemuch and Mundessore, which offices were assailed and gutted.

"The knowledge that other lines of post either existed or would assuredly be established, and that no efforts would be left unemployed to effect free postal intercourse whenever required, possibly pointed to the futility of a general crusade against post runners. Nevertheless, both as a precaution against disappointment and as removing a source of temptation, banghy parcels were discontinued for four months, from July until November.

"The only lines which have been permanently closed are four branch lines in Malwa.

"That no coercion was used, and that the post was kept open (it is true by circuitous routes, but still open) all through this postal range, is strong evidence that the feeling of the country was not unfavourable to British authority; it was found that whenever a road was impracticable, it was rendered so only from fear of the acts of rebels, upon whose departure or overthrow the post line was again opened.

"Exempt as the post carriers have been from concurrence in the general insurrection, the conduct of the other descriptions of postal servants has been not less good, with the exception of those attached to the Indore post office. There the temptation of plunder excited an overseer and peon, and the people of the workshop, to join in plundering the post office and premises, and one kitmutgar (table servant), a Mussulman at Samwere, near Oojein, hounded on some miscreants to murder an European serjeant from Mahidpore, who took refuge in it, for which he was subsequently hanged, and the others transported.

"In the higher grades, the conduct of the postal officers has been very exemplary; no instance has occurred in which a postmaster either deserted his post, or has been suspected of having made use of his position to give information, to open letters, or to favour in any way the rebel cause.

"Ten travellers' bungalows and seven post offices have been burned down, and ten evacuated, of which three only have remained closed. This does not represent the extent of injury done, or loss occasioned, the destruction of stamps, and in other ways by the carrying away of mail carts, destruction of property, and loss in postage collection, and compensation to people in postal employ for good behaviour, or for personal suffering."

The success of the postal arrangements during the Mutiny is largely due to the organization and example of Mr. Riddell, the Director-General, who attended to all important matters personally. He was assisted by the loyal devotion of the entire staff, and the men whose names may be mentioned for special services are Mr.

Dove, officiating Postmaster-General, Bengal; Mr. Bennett, Mr. Wallace and Mr. McGowan, of the Bengal establishment; Lala Salig Ram in the North-Western Provinces; Dr. Clark and Mr. H. A. Brown in Agra; Captain Fanshawe and Babu Eshan Chander Mookerjee in Aligarh; Mr. Taylor in the Deccan and Babu Sheo Pershad in Delhi. Where so many did well it seems invidious to mention only a few names, and the President in Council, when thanking the Director-General for the work done by the Post Office during the crisis, expressed the high opinion which the Government entertained of the services rendered by all the officers of the Department, European and Indian, in circumstances of the greatest difficulty.

Enough has been written to show the nature of the help given to the Indian Empire by the staff of the Post Office during the Mutiny. It is a record of loyalty and devotion to duty of which the Department may well be proud.

CHAPTER XVII

THE INDIAN FIELD POST OFFICE

IN a country where there is seldom perfect peace it is only natural that the Post Office must accustom itself to war conditions, and the Field Postal Service has been a feature of the Indian Post Office for more than sixty years. During that period there have been over forty wars and expeditions, extending from Burma to the Mediterranean, and, as postal arrangements were required for the forces engaged, the Field Post Office system in India has been gradually developed and perfected, and is now recognized as an important part of the military organization of the country.

Field Post Office arrangements used to be in the hands of the Postmaster-General of the Punjab, and he maintained lists of men willing to serve. In 1918, however, owing to the wide distribution of the postal staff in various parts of the world, it was found necessary to bring the Field Post organization under the immediate control of the Director-General. When an expedition is announced, the forces of the Post Office are immediately mobilized according to the strength of the field army, and, as the staff required for a brigade and division has been settled by long experience, no time is lost in getting the necessary number of men to the assembling stations.

The regulations for the working of Field Post Offices

are laid down in the Indian Field Service Manual and the Postal Manual (War), two handbooks issued by the Indian Army Department; and a complete equipment of tents and furniture, sufficient for three base post offices, fifty first-class and twenty second-class field offices, and for the use of the supervisory staff, is kept at Lahore ready for immediate despatch. When the Department has to make its own arrangements for the carriage of mails between the base post office and the field offices, overseers are employed to supervise the transit. The establishment laid down for a base office is one postmaster, two deputy or assistant postmasters, fifteen clerks and ten menials, but these numbers must necessarily vary with the number of field offices required with the different units.

Postal officials in the field are subject to full military discipline under the Army Act. Superior officers wear field service khaki uniform with badges of rank and the letters "Post" in brass on the shoulders. A Deputy Postmaster-General or Assistant Director-General of the Post Office ranks as a Lieutenant-Colonel, and a Superintendent as Major, Captain or Lieutenant, according to his grade and length of service. Subordinate officials, if Europeans, are classed as Assistant Commissaries, Sub-Conductors or Sergeants, according to their pay, and Indians are given rank as Subadars, Jemadars, Havildars or Naiks. Field allowances, in addition to pay, are fixed according to a sanctioned scale, the rate for a Director or Superintendent being 25 per cent of his pay, subject to a minimum monthly allowance of Rs.100 in the case of the latter. Inspectors and Postmasters draw Rs.90 a month in addition to pay, other subordinates being remunerated at a lower rate. In virtue of the military rank held by them, officers and subordinates are entitled to all privileges and advantages for service in the field, such as wound pensions, family pensions, medals and compensation for loss of baggage.

The officer in charge of field post offices is attached to the head-quarters of an Expeditionary Force as adviser to the Military Authorities on all postal matters; he is required to visit the base and field post offices as frequently as possible, and is responsible for the proper working and efficiency of mail arrangements. He arranges with head-quarters for carriage of mails between the base and the field, fixes the hours of despatch of mails from all post offices and the hours during which money orders are issued, and also settles the question of making over cash collections to the nearest Field Paymaster, Treasure Chest Officer, Regimental Accounts Officer or Post Commandant, as the case may be.

The development of the Field Postal System has been gradual and has undergone many changes. The earliest record of a regular Indian Post Office staff proceeding for active service with a military force is in connection with the Persian Expedition of 1856. The establishment consisted of two clerks, an interpreter (moonshee) and four peons, and, as no suitable departmental officer could be found to take charge of the arrangements, the Government of Bombay appointed the Military Paymaster of the Persian Expeditionary Force to take control.

The work accomplished by the Post Office during the Indian Mutiny has been described in a separate chapter. Every office situated within the wide area of the disturbances or on the line of march of the troops performed the functions of a field post office, the control of the arrangements devolving on the chief local civil or military authority in places where there was no departmental officer of sufficient seniority or rank to hold charge. The great services rendered by the Post Office horse transit and bullock train establishments to the Army were a prominent feature of the campaign. Separate field post offices accompanied the moving columns under Generals Havelock, Outram, Campbell, Hugh Rose, Hope Grant and other leaders. Twenty years later, when the Afghan war broke out, the Army had again to rely on the Post Office for the transport of mails and military stores for hundreds of miles through the Khyber and Bolan passes into Afghanistan.

The extension of the railways to the frontiers of India has put an end to this branch of postal enterprise. Mail tonga lines worked by contractors still flourish on routes where there are no railways, but they are being gradually supplanted by motor conveyances.

A scheme under which the Post Office should maintain a large number of motor mail vans, which could be used in time of war for military transport, has already been suggested, and it is one well worth consideration. An arrangement of this kind should go far towards solving the problem of maintaining transport in times of peace, and should prove advantageous and economical to both the Army and the Post Office.

The success of the Indian Field Post Office in the numerous wars and expeditions in which it has been employed can be vouched for by the reports of commanding officers. Experience has been bought by long practice, and the Department never loses an opportunity of training its staff for military service. At the great military manœuvres which are frequently held during the cold weather in India the troops engaged are always accompanied by field post offices fully equipped for war conditions, with the result that there is always a large body of men in the Post Office thoroughly trained in this kind of work. On field service the postal official is "Nobody's child." He has to fend for himself, and, although transport is told off for the conveyance of camp equipment and mails, it is seldom forthcoming when required. The Army Head-quarters Staff looks after its own post office, but is inclined to regard the others as an encumbrance, and this attitude has developed a faculty of "slimness" in the field postal officer, which he uses for defeating military regulations. He has become an expert in stealing transport ; a mule, a cart, a few coolies, a motor lorry, even an idle railway train, all serve his purpose as occasion rises, and his motto is "Get there, if not by fair means, then somehow," and get there he generally does. He has an uncanny instinct for finding out the secret destination of his brigade and is often on the ground, sorting the mail, before the troops arrive.

Mr. Charles Sheridan, a very well-known member of the Department, used to tell an amusing story of the horror of a senior staff officer meeting him one day on a frontier road pronounced absolutely unfit for wheeled traffic. Mr. Sheridan was driving along merrily with the mails in a two-horsed tonga ; it was the shortest road and he took it, and the staff had to reconsider seriously their strategic plans, simply because the Superintendent of the Postal Service would not act according to military instructions.

The heart of the field postal system in any campaign is the Base Office. It is there that all information concerning the movements of regiments and units is carefully recorded. Lists of officers are kept in alphabetical order, and these lists are kept corrected from day to day on information received from the various field offices. The Base Office controls the main routes of mails to the divisional and brigade offices, it issues instructions and is ready to supply reliefs. It searches for missing men, disposes of undeliverable correspondence and has a hospital for repairing articles damaged in transit; in fact, the smooth running of the whole organization depends on the work done at the Base.

The arrangements for conveying the mails between the base office and the field offices devolves on the supervising officers, and endless difficulties have to be faced in order to obtain transport. A great deal depends on the personality of the postal officer in charge. If he is a pleasant fellow and popular with the transport staff he can get most things done, but, if he is insistent on his rights and has not learnt the meaning of "give and take" on a campaign, he will get nothing but excuses and regrets, the mail bags will be left behind in the last camp, irate Colonels will write to their personal friend the Director-General and the promising career of a conscientious public servant will be seriously injured.

In Appendix H is given a list of the most important expeditions in which field post offices have been employed, with a brief account of the arrangements made on each occasion. Most of these were small frontier wars and little difficulty was felt in providing the personnel. The Great War, however, was a very different matter. It necessitated the despatch of large numbers of post offices all over the world, and the demand on the resources of the Post Office of India was on such a vast scale that an account of it has been reserved for a separate chapter.

CHAPTER XVIII

THE INDIAN FIELD POST OFFICE DURING THE GREAT WAR

IN 1914, when war broke out, a large postal contingent accompanied the troops sent to France. It was under the control of Mr. Pilkington, Assistant Director-General of the Post Office, who had the rank of Lieutenant-Colonel, and it comprised one Base Office and 22 field offices, with a staff of 13 supervising officers, 22 field postmasters, 84 clerks and 78 menials. During the early years of the war the work performed by this staff was very heavy. Frequently over 23,000 letters and 2000 parcels would arrive for the Indian contingent in one day, while newspapers published in England were regularly received for delivery to the troops. At the end of 1916 the Indian field postal staff in France was considerably reduced, as large numbers accompanied the Indian troops transferred to Egypt and Mesopotamia, and at the end of the war only one or two field offices remained to serve some Labour Corps units which had been left behind.

At the end of 1916 Mesopotamia was the most important theatre of war so far as the Indian Post Office was concerned. A small field postal contingent was sent in 1914 and was steadily increased as the operations extended. Mr. A. B. Thompson, Deputy Postmaster-General, was the first Director of Postal Services. He was succeeded in 1917 by Mr. A. J. Hughes, who had been Deputy Director in Egypt. By the end of 1917 the army was so large and the work of the Post Office so extensive that it was decided to place an officer of the rank of Postmaster-General in charge, and Mr. H. A. Sams, Postmaster-General, Central Circle, was selected to be Director of Postal Services in Mesopotamia. By 1918 the staff consisted of 17 superintendents, 45 inspectors, 2 base postmasters, 7 deputy postmasters, 79 field postmasters, 542 clerks and 797 menials. The Field Post Office in Mesopotamia had not only military work, but also a great deal of civil work. The magnitude of the business may be gauged by the following monthly figures:—

	ABOUT
Number of letters received and despatched	12,000,000
Number of parcels received and despatched	70,000
Number of money orders issued and paid	67,000
Value of money orders issued and paid	Rs.30,00,000

Large numbers of British postal orders were also sold and Savings Bank business was freely transacted.

During the year 1916 a great deal of difficulty was experienced in Mesopotamia in dealing with returned letters, the addressees of which could not be traced. To dispose of these a Returned Letter Office was established at Basra, for which a staff of 165 permanent base men was employed. Subsequently, as these men were released or recalled to military duty, their places were taken by Anglo-Indian boys recruited in India. The establishment of the Returned Letter Office put a stop to very many complaints regarding loss of letters. The office used to deal with about 200,000 articles a month and worked very efficiently under the supervision of the Base Postmaster, Basra.

Upon the fall of Kut the field post office there shared the fate of the garrison, and a number of postal officials were taken prisoners of war by the Turks.

From the beginning of 1918 to the end of the war the postal service in Mesopotamia was extremely good, and both in Basra and Bagdad a regular local post was established and deliveries by postmen were introduced. At the end of 1918 a number of civil post offices were opened and steps were taken to close down field post offices wherever possible. From the 1st May, 1919, the postal administration of Mesopotamia was finally handed over to the civil authorities and almost all the field post offices were withdrawn, but a very large proportion of the Indian Field staff remained in the country and took service under the new Iraq Government.

Next in importance to Mesopotamia came the Indian postal services in Egypt, Palestine and Salonika, and in these places the Indian field post offices worked side by side with the British Army Postal Corps. In 1915 they were under the control of Mr. A. J. Hughes as Deputy Director, who was succeeded later by Mr. S. C. Sinclair. In 1915 Indian field post offices were sent to Gallipoli, and the work done by them there won the warm appreciation of the military authorities. The extension of operations to Palestine necessitated the despatch of a number of field post offices to that country. In 1918 it was found necessary to separate the postal contingent at Salonika from the control of the Deputy Director in Egypt, and the force was placed in charge of Mr. A.

Gillespie as an independent Assistant Director, with a staff of 1 base postmaster, 2 inspectors, 28 field postmasters and clerks and 36 menials. The Salonika postal service extended to Baku and Constantinople, where there were Indian field post offices.

Field post offices were sent to East Africa in 1914 under the control of Mr. K. A. Appleby, who was subsequently made a Brevet Lieutenant-Colonel. The organization consisted of a base office, 25 field post offices, with a staff of 4 superintendents, 6 inspectors, 1 base postmaster, 25 field postmasters, 76 clerks and 67 menials. About a million letters and parcels were handled monthly by this staff, and work had to be carried on under the most trying conditions, as many of the mail lines traversed country covered with thick jungle. In 1917 and 1918 the whole postal service of German East Africa was carried on by the Indian Field Post Office, and the greatest credit is due to Lieutenant-Colonel Appleby for the excellent arrangements made by him.

In 1918 Lieutenant Kilman was sent to take control of the field post offices attached to the East Persian Cordon between Meshed and Dalbandin. The East Persian Cordon was subsequently known as the Force in East Persia, and the postal organization consisted of 1 Base post office and 13 field post offices, with a staff of an Assistant Director of Posts and Telegraphs, 1 inspector, 1 base postmaster, 13 field postmasters, 31 clerks and 54 menials.

A field post office contingent was also sent to Bushire in 1918 in connection with the operations between Bushire and Shiraz. This was placed under the control of Mr. C. F. Quilter as Assistant Director, who was also given control of the postal arrangements of the British

Mission Escort in South Persia operating from Bunder-Abbas to Kerman and Shiraz. The British Mission Escort commenced its operations early in 1916 and its postal arrangements were in charge of Captain Greene, R.E., Superintendent of post offices, prior to their being taken over by Mr. Quilter. Up to March, 1919, the postal organization of the Bushire Force and British Mission Escort consisted of 2 Base post offices and 18 field post offices, with a staff of an Assistant Director, a Deputy Assistant Director, 2 inspectors, 2 base post-masters, 18 field postmasters, 49 clerks and 86 menials. From April, 1919, the Force was considerably reduced and a large portion of the field postal staff was withdrawn.

The operations in the neighbourhood of Aden led to the establishment of a few field post offices under the postmaster of Aden, who carried out this work in addition to his own.

The total number of officials of the Indian field post offices serving with the various Expeditionary Forces in 1918 was about two thousand, and with this large contingent serving abroad the Department in India had to undertake the difficult task of equipping and despatching regular reinforcements to the several theatres of war. In order to deal with the enormous quantity of Army mails, both originating in India and received from abroad, two special base offices were established, one at Bombay and one at Karachi. The Base Office in Bombay was converted in 1918 into a Base Postal Depot, and in addition to dealing with the mails for the troops it was also assigned the duty of recruitment and mobilization of postal reinforcements. The establishment of the Base Postal Depot in Bombay solved many of the difficulties which attended the organization of field post offices and the disposal of mails for armies in the field. The depot was divided into four main sections for Enquiry, Sorting, Mobilization and Correspondence. The chief duty of the Enquiry section was to ensure the correct delivery of correspondence for the troops that had returned or had been invalided from the field. This section was in charge of a lady Superintendent with forty lady clerks, and their duty was to keep up to date a regular record giving the names, designations and addresses of officers and men who had returned to India. The Enquiry section kept its records by means of index cards, of which there were over 133,000 when the armistice was declared. About 330,000 letters monthly were disposed of in this section.

In the Sorting section the average number of postal articles dealt with in a month was about one million. The sorting of mails for all the forces was done by units, separate bundles or packets being prepared for the officers and men with each unit. These mails were then forwarded ready sorted to the base offices at the various fronts, where they were distributed to the field offices serving the units in question.

The Mobilization section dealt with all matters relating to the mobilization of the staff recruited in India for service overseas. Only men who had volunteered for field service were taken, and on receiving orders these men reported themselves to the Officer Commanding, Base Postal Depot, Bombay, who arranged for their kit, uniform and transport to the force for which they were detailed. The Correspondence section dealt with all complaints regarding postal articles for the field forces, and, by being in close connection with the Enquiry branch, it was able to dispose of a large number of complaints without delay.

The Base Postal Depot, Bombay, was thus the most essential factor in the whole postal organization, and the smooth working of mail arrangements for the Expeditionary Forces depended very largely upon its efficiency. The Depot was directly under the control of the Director-General of Posts and Telegraphs and in charge of Captain Love, a pensioned officer of the Department, who had retired as Presidency Postmaster, Bombay.

To reward the good work done by the Indian postal staff in the field, no less than fifty-two personal distinctions were granted and over three hundred men were mentioned in despatches. The Department may well be proud of its achievements during the war. Volunteers were always ready to come forward for service in the worst places and many lost their lives. The best proof of their work, however, is the high reputation which the Post Office of India has earned among all branches of the Army.

CHAPTER XIX

INDIAN POSTAGE STAMPS

THE first issue of postage stamps in India was made by Sir Bartle Frere in the Province of Scinde (now spelt Sind) in 1852. At that time the post offices of Scinde were administered by the Local Government, and it was not until 1855 that they were placed under the control of the Postmaster-General of Bombay. The Scinde District dawk stamps are very rare. There were three kinds: (1) the design embossed on white paper without colour; (2) blue embossed on white paper; (3) the design embossed on vermilion wafers. The design is shown in the accompanying illustration (Fig. 1), and the central portion consists of a modification of the broad arrow used by the East India Company. The issue was a comparatively small one, and the stamps were withdrawn from use in September, 1854.

The early postal system of India was solely used for official purposes, and it was not until 1837 that a public post was established. Postage rates varied with distance, and the charge was levied in cash, the lowest rate being two annas for every hundred miles. For this purpose copper tokens of the value of two annas were struck which were available for the prepayment of postage.

In 1850 a Commission was appointed to inquire into the working of the Post Office, and among its recom-

FIG. 1

FIG. 2

FIG. 3

On

H M

S

FIG. 4

EARLY STAMPS

mendations were the formation of an Imperial Post Office of India under a Director-General, the abolition of franking and the employment of stamps in prepayment of postage.

There was a great deal of discussion between the Indian Government and the Court of Directors in London as to where the stamps should be manufactured; the former desired to procure them from England, but the latter, on the ground of economy, decided that sufficiently good stamps could be made in India. The first effort was a design of the "Lion and Palm tree" made by Colonel Forbes of the Calcutta Mint. This essay (Fig. 2), however, was never used, as the Mint could not promise a sufficient supply. Subsequently the manufacture of stamps was entrusted to the Survey Office, and after many failures Captain Thuillier, Deputy Surveyor-General, succeeded in producing nine hundred sheets of red half-anna stamps by means of lithography. These stamps are known as the red ½ anna stamps "with 9½ arches" and were printed in sheets of one hundred and twenty, consisting of twelve rows of ten labels. They were sent to Bombay on the 5th April, 1854, but after despatch it was found that the stock of vermilion was exhausted, and as the same quality of ink could not be procured in India a new ink was prepared and at the same time a fresh design was made. Owing to the fresh design, it was decided not to issue the "9½ arches" stamps. It is disappointing to think that this first and historic set of Indian stamps was never used postally; but the omission does not seem to have detracted from their philatelic value. Good specimens are very rare, and command a high price in the market.

The design for the ½ anna stamp that was finally

accepted was one of eight arches, and it was printed in blue. There are three distinct shades of blue in the 1854 issues, varying from deep to pale. These stamps were prepared by engraving on copper plate and transferring to stones. The sheets consisted of twelve horizontal rows of eight stamps on paper watermarked with the arms of the East India Company. The sheets, dated May and July, 1854, were evidently made up of blocks of twenty-four stamps, repeated four times on each sheet. This is apparent from the fact that the fifth stamp in each of the third, sixth, ninth and twelfth rows is slightly out of alignment, and the sixth stamp in each of the first, fourth, seventh and ninth rows has had the chignon redrawn (Plate facing p. 180). The sheets are not perforated, and are without gum: 333,399 sheets were printed in 1854 and 48,831 in 1855.

The 1 anna stamp was printed in vermilion-red, and 26,897 sheets were ready by August, 1854; there were further supplies of 54,961 sheets in November, 1854, and 15,834 sheets by November, 1855.

The colour selected for the 2 annas stamp was green, and the printing was completed in October, 1854. There is no record of the number printed.

The need for a 4 annas stamp was badly felt for postage to the United Kingdom, which cost 1 rupee 4 annas an ounce in 1854. A design was prepared in two colours, blue and red, and the first sheets contained only twelve stamps (Plate facing p. 178), and the first supply consisted of 17,170 sheets delivered on 14th October, 1854; in all 61,580 sheets were printed. In April, 1855, a new setting was adopted with twenty-four stamps on a sheet, and two arrangements of this setting were made, one with the stamps much closer together than the other.

BLOCK SHOWING ONE THIRD OF A SHEET OF BLUE HALF ANNA STAMPS OF 1854. PRINTED IN CALCUTTA

All the stamps referred to above were prepared by Captain Thuillier, who subsequently became General Sir Henry Thuillier, C.S.I., Surveyor-General of India.

In November, 1855, stamps of the value of ½, 1, 2, 4 and 8 annas were received from Messrs. De La Rue & Co. The designs were engraved on steel and the stamps were printed on white wove unwatermarked paper with white gum. The 4 and 8 annas are also found printed on a highly glazed thick bluish paper without watermark. These stamps supplanted the old issues manufactured in India, but the stocks of the latter were not finally called in and destroyed until 1858.

In 1860 8 pies[1] stamps were on sale in India. These were required for prepayment of soldiers' letters to the United Kingdom. Up to August, 1855, British soldiers' correspondence was carried free of charge, but when this privilege was withdrawn they had the option of prepaying the postage in cash at 9 pies a tola (⅜ of an ounce) or else affixing a stamp for 8 pies. Up to 1864 certain changes were made in the colours of some of these stamps; the 2 annas green was altered to brown-pink early in 1856, subsequently to buff, and then to yellow. At the end of 1864 the colour of the 4 annas was changed from black to green, as the stamp had been forged.

The 8 annas and 4 annas stamps on bluish glazed paper, and the 4 annas, 1 anna and 8 pies on white paper, have been found cut in halves upon postal articles in order to pay half their face value postage. All covers found with these bisected stamps were posted in Singapore, which had an Indian post office at the time.

The first issue of Indian postage stamps with the

[1] 12 pies = 1 anna = 1 penny approximately.

elephant's head watermarked was made in 1866. The values bearing this watermark are ½ anna, 8 pies, 1 anna, 2 annas 9 pies, 4 annas, 6 annas, 6 annas 8 pies, 12 annas, 1 rupee.

The 6 annas 8 pies stamps were printed as this was the rate per ounce for letters to the United Kingdom via Marseilles between 1863 and 1874. The stamps, however, were not actually issued until 1867, and their sale was discontinued in 1874, when the Marseilles route was abandoned.

Up to 1882 all the Indian stamps printed in London were of smaller size than English stamps, and they bore the inscription "EAST INDIA POSTAGE." In 1882 new dies on a larger scale were prepared by Messrs. De La Rue, and the inscription was changed to "INDIA POSTAGE." The values issued were ½ anna 9 pies, 1 anna, 1 anna 6 pies, 2 annas, 3 annas, 4 annas, 4 annas 6 pies, 8 annas, 12 annas, 1 rupee. The stamps were printed on medium white wove paper watermarked with a five-pointed star.

On 1st January, 1891, the postage to the United Kingdom was reduced to 2 annas and 6 pies, and a new stamp was prepared. Until the new issue was ready the 4 annas 6 pies stamps were surcharged with "2½ As." Bi-coloured stamps of 1 rupee, 2 rupees, 3 rupees and 5 rupees were also printed and a provisional 3 pies stamp was issued, made by surcharging the ½ anna stamp with "¼" in black. The stamps of 2, 3 and 5 rupees were of specially large size and bore a later portrait of the Queen (Fig. 3). This portrait was also adopted for the 3 pies carmine stamp which was issued in 1899. Owing to the decision of the Postal Union to have uniform colours for stamps representing the initial rates of international postages the colours of the ½ anna, 1 anna and 2 annas

SPECIMEN VICTORIAN ISSUES

6 pies stamps were changed to yellow-green, carmine and ultramarine. This necessitated a change in the 3 pies from carmine to grey and in the 2 annas from ultramarine to mauve.

The King Edward VII issues of 1902–3 were of the same corresponding values as those of the Queen Victoria stamps 1882–1900. The colours are 3 pies, grey ; ½ anna, yellow-green ; 1 anna, carmine ; 2 annas, mauve ; 2 annas 6 pies, ultramarine ; 3 annas, orange-brown ; 4 annas, olive-green ; 6 annas, bistre ; 8 annas, purple ; 12 annas, purple on red paper ; 1 rupee, green and carmine ; 2 rupees, carmine and yellow-brown ; 3 rupees brown and green ; 5 rupees, ultramarine and violet.

In 1906 it was decided to abolish the special receipt stamp and to use the ½ anna and 1 anna postage stamp for both postage and revenue purposes. A new design was therefore prepared for these values with the inscription "INDIA POSTAGE AND REVENUE."

In 1909 the double-headed telegraph stamps were abolished and it was decided to employ postage stamps in payment of telegrams. The value of telegraph stamps extended to fifty rupees, but it was considered sufficient to add three new values to the postage stamps for use upon the more expensive telegrams, namely 10, 15 and 25 rupees. These stamps are of the same size and design as the 2, 3 and 5 rupees issues, and the colours are 10 rupees, pink and green ; 15 rupees, olive-brown and blue ; 25 rupees, orange and blue.

The stamps of George V issued in 1911 were completely re-designed. The higher values with the elephants as supporters are very artistic. In 1913 the 2 annas 6 pies stamp was re-designed and the colour changed from ultramarine to bright blue.

In 1918 the United Kingdom raised the postage rate to India from 1d. to 1½d., and, to correspond with the increase, the Government of India raised the postage to the United Kingdom to 1½ annas. The new stamp was intended to be a dark chocolate-brown, but was printed by Messrs. De La Rue & Co. in a light chocolate.

In 1866 service postage stamps first came into use for employment on official correspondence. The ½ anna, 1 anna, 2 annas and 4 annas were overprinted with the word "Service." The first supply was overprinted in India pending the arrival of the stamps ordered from England. A consignment of 8 annas overprinted was also received from England. In 1874 the overprint was altered to "On H. M. S.," as shown in Fig. 4, and in 1883 the rupee stamp was also overprinted in this way.

Various other overprints were used by local bodies in India, but after a time the practice was forbidden. In 1911 the overprint was again altered to "Service."

The following overprints were also used for Indian postage in other countries:

Straits Settlements .	1867–1868, Queen's Head.
Zanzibar	1895–1896 „
British East Africa .	„ „
C.E.F. (China Expeditionary Force) . .	1900 to present date.
British Somaliland .	1903–1904, Queen's and King's Head.
I.E.F. (Indian Expeditionary Force) . .	1914 to present date.

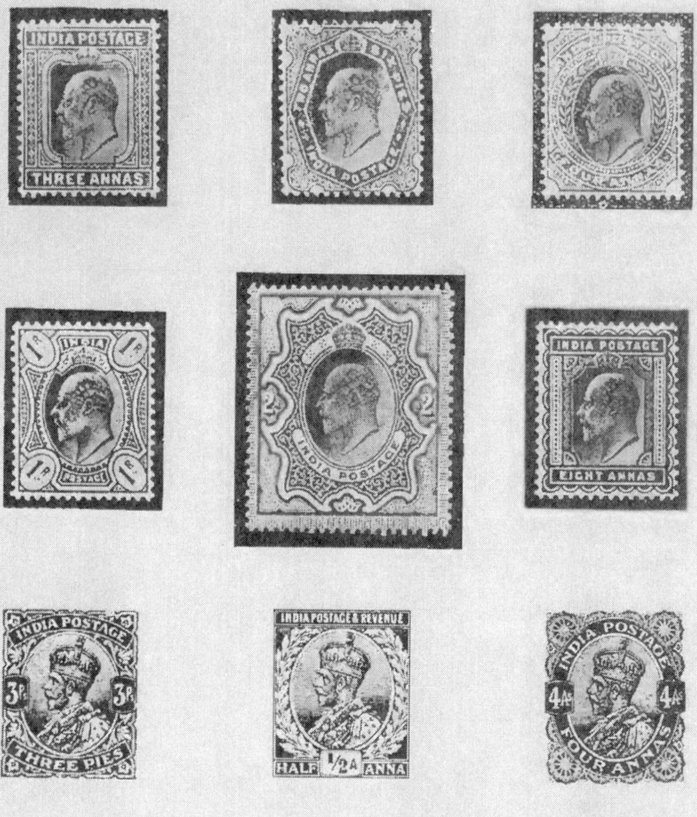

SPECIMEN EDWARDIAN AND GEORGIAN ISSUES

Overprints (Indian Convention States)

Patiala	1884 to present date.
Gwalior	1885 ,,
Jhind	,, ,,
Nabha	,, ,,
Faridkot	1886–1901.
Chamba	1896 to present date.

There are many varieties of the overprints in the Indian Convention States stamps and many errors, which have led to numerous forgeries of the different overprints.

A very exhaustive history of the postage stamps of India with detailed accounts of errors and provisional issues will be found in *The Postage and Telegraph Stamps of British India*, by L. L. R. Hausburg, C. Stewart Wilson and C. S. F. Crofton, published by Messrs. Stanley Gibbons. This is the standard work on the subject, and it contains many fine plates and illustrations. Part I, on postage stamps, is written by Mr. Hausburg, and no article on Indian stamps can pretend to be anything more than a résumé of his detailed researches.

One merit the Postal Administration of India can justly claim and that is the purity of its stamp issues. The simple design of the Sovereign's head has always been maintained and the temptation to issue fancy pictures for commemoration purposes has always been steadily avoided.

APPENDICES

APPENDIX A

PERSONNEL OF THE POST OFFICE

THE following table gives the staff of the Department on the 1st April, 1919 :—

Controlling Staff . .	88
General Supervising Staff .	747
Postmasters . . .	7,041
Extra Departmental Agents .	12,668
Clerical and Signalling Staff .	24,620
Postmen and Peons . .	43,768
Road Establishment . .	18,467
Linemen	2,959
Total . . .	110,358

The Audit Staff of the Posts and Telegraphs has not been included as this is under the control of the Finance Department.

Recruitment for the posts of Superintendent is effected in two ways, namely—

(1) by the selection of qualified persons not already in the service of the Department, and
(2) by the promotion of officials from the subordinate ranks of the Department.

In the former case the person selected is generally required to join as a probationary superintendent, and is not given a permanent appointment until he has shown his fitness in every respect for the position and has passed an examination in Post Office work.

Ordinarily a probationary superintendent is not allowed to act as a superintendent until he has had a practical training in postal work; that is to say, he performs the duties of a postmaster, accompanies a superintendent on tour and is given an insight into the general working of the Department in the offices of the Postmaster-General and Superintendent. There is no minimum period fixed in which a probationer, when fully qualified, must receive a permanent post. It depends on the vacancies that occur in the sanctioned cadre; but experience has shown that the period seldom exceeds two and a half years, and the average is two years and two months.

Postmasters are generally recruited from the lower ranks of the Department, such as sub-postmasters and clerks, who usually start their careers as probationers. The exceptions to this rule are the probationary postmasters, who are specially selected in order to improve the personnel in the higher appointments.

APPENDIX B

EXTRACTS FROM EARLY REGULATIONS REGARDING THE MAIL SERVICE

AN extract from the Consultations, 17th January, 1774, gives in detail the arrangement made by Warren Hastings for the improvement of postal arrangements.

The President lays down before the Board the following plan for the better regulations of the Dauks and for forming a General Post Office :—

The present management of the Dauks is attended with many inconveniences. Private letters are exempt from postage and the whole expense of the establishment falls upon the Company. The Dauks from the same cause are loaded with packages of the most frivolous kind and of unreasonable weights. The privilege of sending private letters by the Dauks being confined to the European inhabitants, affords but a partial aid to the necessary intercourse of trade. The establishment is branched out into various departments, all independent and unconnected, the expense partly defrayed by ready-money payments and partly by taxes on the zemindars and farmers, who make an advantage of them in the deductions of their rents. From all these causes the establishment is involved in a labyrinth of obscurity, without checks and without system. The delays on the road are often greater than those of common cossids or couriers without a possibility of correcting them, because it cannot be known by whom they are occasioned. Of these delays the President himself has had repeated proofs insomuch that whenever he has had occasion for extraordinary despatch he has made use of express cossids, and these never failed to exceed the regular Dauks by nearly half the space of time employed by the latter for the same distance. The loose and irregular manner in which the letters are received and distributed exposes the correspondence of individuals and even the public despatches to great delays and to the risk of being lost or intercepted.

To remedy these evils, the following plan is submitted to the Board, for the future management of this office, in which it is attempted to limit the expense to provide a fund for its support by laying a moderate postage on private letters, to render it of more extensive use and to form the different parts into one uniform and general system.

Plan of a new Establishment of Dauks and of a General Post Office

1. That the Dauks be formed into four divisions as follows :—

First Division from Calcutta to Ganjam ;
Second Division from Calcutta to Patna ;
Third Division from Patna to Benares and to such farther distance as may be hereafter determined ;
Fourth Division from Calcutta to Dacca.

2. That no Dauks be appointed to the cross-roads (excepting Dinagepur) as hereafter mentioned, but cossids only occasionally employed by the Provincial Councils and Collectors to convey the letters to the nearest stages of the Dauks ; the pay and other charges of these cossids to be transmitted monthly to the Postmaster-General, whose office will be hereafter described.

3. That as the military operations in Cooch Behar require a constant and regular correspondence, a cross-post be established between Dinagepur and Rajmehal, and that it remains for future consideration whether it will be necessary to establish a cross-post from Burdwan on the assembling of the Council at that place.

4. That three hercarrahs or dauks, one massalchy [1] and one drum be appointed to each stage, viz. :

[1] Torchbearer.

	Miles.	Furl.	Stages.	Harcrs.	Massl.	Drum.
From Calcutta to Ganjam	358	2	42	126	42	42
„ Calcutta to Patna .	398	6	48	144	48	48
„ Patna to Benares .	165	4	19	57	19	19
„ Calcutta to Dacca .	179	4	21	63	21	21
Cross-road from Dinagepur to Rajmehal . . .	77	2	9	27	9	9
	1179	2	139	417	139	139

5. That a Munshi be fixed at each capital stage who shall have charge of a certain number of stages.

6. That two gurreewallas or time-keepers be appointed with each Munshi for the purpose of determining the arrival of each packet, which shall be written on the outside of the packet and an account thereof with the time of the last despatch kept by the Munshi.

7. That a deputy postmaster be appointed with the following establishment of servants at the following stations, who shall have charge of all the stages from the Presidency to the place of his residence, pay the Munshi's charges dependent on him, take an account of all letters received and despatched, receive and issue letters, transmit his accounts and reports to the Postmaster-General, and receive his orders :—

Establishment at	Deputy.	Peons.
Moorshedabad	1	10
Patna	1	10
Benares	1	2
Ganjam	1	2
Dacca	1	2
Dinagepur	1	2
	6	28

8. That a Postmaster-General be appointed at Calcutta with one Deputy, one merda or native assistant, seven sorters, one jemadar and fifteen peons for distributing letters. He will have the control of the whole establishment, and all the accounts will be brought into his office.

Bye-Rules

1. That all letters shall pay postage, excepting such as are on the public service.

2. That the postage on inland letters shall be paid when put into the office at the following rates :—

> Single letters for every 100 miles, 2 annas. Double letters in proportion according to their weight.

3. That letters coming by sea, or from foreign settlements, shall pay on delivery and be rated at half postage.

4. That a table of postage, formed according to the above rules, be affixed at the different offices for the public inspection.

5. That the post office in Calcutta shall be open from 10 o'clock in the morning till 1 for the delivery of letters, and from 6 till 9 in the evening for the receipt of letters.

6. That a daily account of the number and weight of letters despatched, with the amount of postage, be kept at each office, that a monthly account be transmitted to the Postmaster-General by his Deputies and that a general abstract of the whole receipts and disbursements be laid before the Board every month.

7. That the letters when received into the offices shall be sorted and put up in separate bags for the different stations, together with a note of the number in each.

8. That all letters shall be stamped with the day of the month on which they are delivered into any chief office.

9. That for the facility of paying the postage on letters small copper tickets be immediately struck to be received at the rate of 2 annas each, but to pass only at the post office.

APPENDIX C

METHODS OF TRAVEL IN EARLY DAYS

THE dak or travelling system prevailing in India in the year 1857 was almost wholly arranged by the Post Office and was available for private individuals as well as for officials. When a traveller contemplated a journey he applied to the local postmaster for means of transport, giving, as a rule, two or three days' previous notice. Horse daks, i.e. wheeled conveyances drawn by horses, were available only on the great trunk roads, which were metalled. On other roads, the journey, when not performed on horseback, was accomplished in a palanquin or palkee, a kind of wooden box, about six feet in length by four in height, fitted at the sides with sliding shutters and suspended on two poles borne on the shoulders of four men. The pleasures of travelling in this fashion have been described by Bishop Heber and other writers. The traveller provided his own palanquin, and the postmaster supplied the palkee-burdars or palanquin-bearers, eight in number, as well as two mussalchees or torchbearers and two bhangy-burdars or luggage porters. The charges, about one shilling per mile for the entire set of twelve men, had to be paid in advance, the traveller notifying the time and place of starting and the duration and localities of halts. There was also an extra charge for demurrage or delays on the road attributable to the traveller himself. For these charges the postmaster undertook that there should be relays of dak servants throughout the whole distance, and, to ensure this, he had to write in advance to the different villages and post stations ordering relays to be ready at the appointed hours. The stages averaged ten miles each and were accomplished in three hours, at the end of which time the twelve men retraced their steps, having been succeeded by another twelve; for each set of men belonged to a particular station. The horse daks were established on the same system, several pairs of horses or ponies being kept at the different stages as relays. The bullock train, which was intended chiefly for baggage and parcels, was largely used for conveyance of troops during the Mutiny. There were one or two private companies in existence, but the public as a rule preferred to use the Government vehicles, as they were considered more reliable.

There were no hotels or inns on the road, but dak bungalows or rest houses, a convenient substitute, were established at places varying from fifteen to fifty miles apart, according as the road was much or little frequented. These bungalows were under Government control, a khidmatgar or servant and a porter being in attendance at each, the traveller paying a fixed sum for the use of his room and making a separate bargain for any few articles of provisions that might be obtainable. The building was little more than a thatched house of one story, divided into two or three rooms, to each of which a bathroom was attached. The khidmatgar cooked and served the meals ordered, while the porter supplied wood and water. The dak system was perfected by Lord Dalhousie, during whose administration many fine metalled roads, including the grand trunk road from Calcutta to the Punjab, were completed. The new system was a great improvement upon the primitive arrangements in force during the Punjab campaign of 1846, when, owing to the tedious nature of the journey and the slow method of progress, out of one hundred officers sent off by palanquin from Calcutta to aid Viscount Hardinge only thirty arrived at the Sutlej before the campaign was over.

APPENDIX D

STATEMENT SHOWING THE WORK OF THE POST OFFICE SAVINGS BANK FROM 1882 TO 1918

Year.	No. of Banks.	No. of Accounts.	Balance. Rs.
1882–83 . . .	4,238	39,121	27,96,796
1883–84 . . .	5,199	84,848	75,14,455
1884–85 . . .	5,499	122,599	1,34,41,911
1885–86 . . .	5,833	155,009	2,25,45,891
1886–87 . . .	6,048	219,010	4,25,19,345
1887–88 . . .	5,966	261,157	5,04,88,357
1888–89 . . .	6,056	311,001	5,88,64,681
1889–90 . . .	6,350	358,272	5,86,96,755
1890–91 . . .	6,455	408,544	6,34,67,408
1891–92 . . .	6,452	463,453	7,05,93,160
1892–93 . . .	6,408	520,967	7,81,87,727
1893–94 . . .	6,358	574,050	8,26,57,319
1894–95 . . .	6,384	611,947	8,40,17,923
1895–96 . . .	6,343	653,892	9,04,23,072
1896–97 . . .	6,420	713,320	9,63,92,411
1897–98 . . .	6,290	730,387	9,28,72,978
1898–99 . . .	6,310	755,871	9,42,80,041
1899–1900 . . .	6,479	785,729	9,64,64,466
1900–01 . . .	6,636	816,651	10,04,32,569
1901–02 . . .	7,053	866,693	10,68,21,233
1902–03 . . .	7,075	922,353	11,42,15,534
1903–04 . . .	7,372	987,635	12,33,36,717
1904–05 . . .	7,855	1,058,813	13,40,70,130
1905–06 . . .	8,071	1,115,758	13,99,26,260
1906–07 . . .	8,049	1,190,220	14,76,69,789
1907–08 . . .	8,328	1,262,763	15,18,14,343
1908–09 . . .	8,501	1,318,632	15,23,41,514
1909–10 . . .	8,767	1,378,916	15,86,71,786
1910–11 . . .	8,929	1,430,451	16,91,88,224
1911–12 . . .	9,502	1,500,834	18,89,85,438
1912–13 . . .	9,460	1,566,860	20,61,14,502
1913–14 . . .	9,824	1,638,725	23,16,75,467
1914–15 . . .	10,161	1,644,074	14,89,26,323
1915–16 . . .	10,386	1,660,424	15,32,12,517
1916–17 . . .	10,421	1,647,419	16,59,53,401
1917–18 . . .	10,975	1,637,600	16,58,46,470

APPENDIX E

STATEMENT OF INLAND MONEY ORDERS ISSUED IN INDIA SINCE 1880

	Number and amount of Ordinary Money Orders issued in India.		Number and amount of Revenue Money Orders issued in India.		Number and amount of Rent Money Orders issued in India.	
Year.	Number.	Value.	Number.	Value.	Number.	Value.
1880–81 . .	1,604,174	4,57,08,580	—	—	—	—
1881–82 . .	2,157,796	5,73,32,026	—	—	—	—
1882–83 . .	2,565,904	6,46,84,182	—	—	—	—
1883–84 . .	3,034,894	7,31,24,179	—	—	—	—
1884–85 . .	3,550,257	8,20,88,559	13,914	3,35,904	—	—
1885–86 . .	4,163,078	9,38,27,375	39,768	7,11,117	—	—
1886–87 . .	4,821,117	10,68,49,151	66,204	11,29,415	—	—
1887–88 . .	5,512,395	11,84,43,572	138,687	20,38,586	1,213	12,358
1888–89 . .	6,136,790	12,99,06,864	196,037	26,83,469	30,165	3,55,283
1889–90 . .	6,759,116	14,65,32,147	262,585	34,70,576	39,823	5,25,217
1890–91 . .	7,326,065	15,77,70,303	278,075	41,95,716	58,127	7,42,284
1891–92 . .	7,783,296	16,44,09,526	300,336	44,27,796	78,421	9,74,272
1892–93 . .	8,237,855	17,19,16,585	320,651	49,21,950	99,973	13,01,721
1893–94 . .	8,754,940	18,35,34,008	335,933	50,49,372	110,198	14,37,050
1894–95 . .	9,422,105	19,43,09,308	348,178	56,27,613	119,952	15,84,581
					113,266	15,61,021

1895–96 . .	10,055,036	20,62,03,368	371,806	59,64,630	111,594	15,37,883
1896–97 . .	10,947,571	21,97,28,206	346,510	58,23,851	102,875	14,68,352
1897–98 . .	11,664,350	24,23,37,096	382,402	67,91,786	110,324	15,98,602
1898–99 . .	11,740,565	24,54,50,445	441,034	81,37,197	121,987	17,31,680
1899–00 . .	12,505,059	25,62,50,323	441,739	78,00,682	124,155	18,15,998
1900–01 . .	12,922,465	26,27,19,976	453,862	82,83,758	134,977	19,72,389
1901–02 . .	13,581,928	26,84,51,162	471,387	91,96,336	153,800	22,47,435
1902–03 . .	15,311,955	27,82,17,678	530,778	95,72,448	167,711	23,67,739
1903–04 . .	16,470,115	29,43,59,136	579,851	1,06,87,532	192,375	25,88,723
1904–05 . .	17,657,917	31,04,28,794	692,705	1,04,12,346	192,926	25,83,483
1905–06 . .	19,622,437	33,14,36,803	724,747	1,00,03,341	199,754	26,70,518
1906–07 . .	20,923,383	35,25,97,091	690,688	97,26,046	203,157	27,93,647
1907–08 . .	22,109,666	37,97,08,358	622,501	94,67,041	176,195	23,80,811
1908–09 . .	23,132,115	39,19,26,114	685,021	1,11,10,709	198,683	26,89,768
1909–10 . .	23,888,149	39,96,74,848	740,776	1,16,93,227	219,651	29,82,614
1910–11 . .	24,781,847	41,85,13,444	750,777	1,24,17,561	222,747	29,87,628
1911–12 . .	26,322,257	44,29,23,702	754,306	1,23,49,182	226,982	30,39,792
1912–13 . .	28,624,470	47,39,38,492	754,766	1,21,77,802	252,618	34,27,203
1913–14 . .	29,940,631	51,18,35,732	764,673	1,20,02,271	240,662	32,74,757
1914–15 . .	29,317,377	51,54,81,941	863,235	1,24,31,425	247,468	33,21,068
1915–16 . .	31,281,231	53,92,17,506	844,742	1,36,70,463	261,667	36,73,409
1916–17 . .	32,331,652	57,54,48,259	839,506	1,38,59,594	274,990	37,94,479
1917–18 . .	33,903,625	62,77,87,899	880,700	1,50,47,255	268,419	36,15,440

APPENDIX F

HISTORICAL ASSOCIATIONS OF THE CALCUTTA GENERAL POST OFFICE

THIS handsome building is situated on the west side of Dalhousie Square at the corner of Koila Ghat Street, being a portion of the site of the old Fort of Calcutta. The removal of the old foundations was a work of great difficulty owing to the extreme hardness of the masonry, which in many cases had to be blasted away. The building was erected from designs by Mr. Walter B. Granville, Architect to the Government of India. It was opened to the public in the year 1868 and cost 6,30,000 rupees. It consists of two lofty storys, the east and south fronts being faced with tall Corinthian columns flanked by massive piers in which are the staircases. The south-east angle of the building is semicircular, also faced with Corinthian columns leading to a lofty circular hall in which are the public counters. This is surmounted by a lantern crowned by a dome, which forms a conspicuous object in the city.

The site of the General Post Office is of great historical interest owing to its association with the great tragedy of the Black Hole of Calcutta. On entering the Post Office courtyard from Koila Ghat Street there are two tablets with the following inscriptions :—

I. The brass lines in the stone,
on the adjacent ground,
mark the position and extent
of the South Curtain
of old Fort William.

GENERAL POST OFFICE. CALCUTTA

BLACK HOLE, CALCUTTA.
ADJOINING THE GENERAL POST OFFICE

II. The two lines of twelve arches
to the west of this tablet
are all that now remains above ground
of old Fort William and
originally formed a portion of the arcade
within the South Curtain.
The Black Hole Prison was a small room
formed by bricking up two arches
of a similar but smaller arcade
within the East Curtain
south of the East Gate.

The sunken arches, where the Post Office vans were kept, once formed part of the arcade within the south curtain, the wall line of which is marked out by brass lines let into the pavement. The wall of the curtain, a portion of which was still standing in 1895, backed the old export and import warehouses, and through the arches one would have in the old days looked into the parade ground within the Fort. The export and import warehouses were built against the south curtain in 1741 and would have followed the line of Koila Ghat Street.

The angle of the south-east bastion and the thickness of its walls is indicated by brass lines let into the steps of the Post Office. A tablet pointing out this fact is on the adjacent wall, and the entrance to the east gate of the Fort is commemorated by a tablet fixed into the red building opposite the Holwell obelisk :

Sixteen feet behind this wall
was the entrance of the East Gate
of old Fort William through which
the bodies of those who perished
in the Black Hole were brought and
thrown into the ditch of the Ravelin
on 21st June, 1756.

To the north of the General Post Office building, inside the large gateway, is a tablet with the following inscription :—

THE BLACK HOLE.

The marble pavement below this spot
was placed here
by
Lord Curzon, Viceroy and Governor-General of India,
in 1901
To mark the site of the prison in Old Fort William
known as the Black Hole.
In which 146 British Inhabitants of Calcutta were
confined on the night of the 20th June, 1756,
and from which only 23 came out alive.
The pavement marks the exact breadth of the prison,
14 ft. 10 in., but not its full length, 18 feet.
About one-third of the area at the north end being
covered by the building on which this tablet is erected.

Near by Mr. Holwell, then Collector of Calcutta, who was one of the survivors, erected an obelisk at his own expense to the memory of those who perished in the Black Hole on the spot where the 123 killed were buried. The tablet bore the following inscriptions :—

To the Memory of—

Edward Eyre, William Bailie, Esqrs.; the Revd.
Jervas Bellamy ; Messrs. Jenks, Reeveley, Law, Coates,
Napcourt, Jebb, Torrians, E. Page, S. Page, Grub, Street,
Harod, P. Johnstone, Ballard, N. Drake, Carse, Knapton,
Goslin, Dod, Dalrymple ; Captains Clayton, Buchanan, and
Witherington ; Lieutenants Bishop, Hays, Blagge, Simpson,
and J. Bellamy ; Ensigns Paccard, Scott, Hastings,
C. Wedderburn, and Dymbleton ; Sea-Captains Hunt, Osburn,
and Purnell ; Messrs. Carey, Leech, Stevenson, Guy Porter,
Parker, Caulkee, Bendal and Atkinson ;
Who, with sundry other inhabitants, Military and
Militia, to the number of 123 persons, were, by
the tyrannic violence of Suraj-ud-Dowlah,
Suba of Bengal,

Suffocated in the Black-Hole Prison of Fort William,
on the night of the 20th day of June, 1756,
and promiscuously thrown the succeeding
morning into the ditch
of the ravelin of this place.
This monument is erected by their surviving fellow-sufferer,
J. Z. Holwell.
This horrid act of violence was as amply as deservedly
revenged on Suraj-ud-Dowlah, by His Majesty's arms,
under the conduct of Vice-Admiral Watson and Col. Clive,
Anno 1757.

The Marquis of Hastings in 1840 had the monument pulled down, but Lord Curzon in 1903 had a replica made and placed in the same spot where it now stands.

APPENDIX G

Extract from the narrative of the interruption in the mail arrangements in the N.-W.P. and Punjab subsequent to the Mutiny at Meerut and Delhi on the 10th and 11th May, 1857.

By Mr. G. Paton, Postmaster-General, North-West Provinces.

ON the mutiny of the native troops at Meerut and Delhi on the 10th and 11th May, 1857, the mail communication between Meerut, Delhi and Allyghur was interrupted. The eastern mails were then forwarded from Allyghur via Anoopshahur and Moradabad to Meerut and thence direct to Kurnaul or via Seharanpore to Umballa. In like manner the mails from the north-west were forwarded from Kurnaul and Umballa to Allyghur. There was delay by the arrangement, but it was the only one practicable on the route via Delhi being closed by the mutiny and rebellion there.

2. After the lapse of a week the mail was reopened between Allyghur and Meerut, but by the mutiny of the 9th Regiment N.I. on the 20th June at Allyghur all postal communication from the north, the south, the east and west of that station was stopped.

3. Exertions were made to establish communication between Cawnpore and Meerut via Futtehgurh, Bareilly and Moradabad. Mails were forwarded towards Bareilly, but none issued from or through that station. This excited much uneasiness for some time, but was explained by the mutiny of the troops there and at Shajehanpore on the 30th June. Bareilly was, like Delhi, the scene of the political intrigue, and the suppression of postal communication was there, as elsewhere, an object of the first importance with the insurgents.

4. The post offices and mail lines in Oude, generally, became disorganized about the same time as in Rohilcund, as the troops mutinied almost simultaneously in both provinces.

5. While the Grand Trunk Road between Cawnpore and Agra was open, arrangements were made to maintain communication between the Punjab and Cis-Sutledge States with Agra via Kurnaul Hansie and Jeypore, but the mutiny of the Hurrianah Battalion and a portion of the 4th Irregular Cavalry at Hansie and Hissar in the end of May entirely stopped that line.

6. An attempt was made to open communication with Agra and Meerut via Muttra and by a line midway between Khoorjah and Secunderabad, but it had to be abandoned owing to the rebel Wulleedad Khan and his followers having obtained undisputed possessions of the district of Bulundshahur.

7. But, although Bolundshahur and a large portion of Allyghur were occupied by the rebel Wulleedad Khan, a line of runners was established between Meerut and Agra via Gurhmooktesur Ghat, the left bank of the Ganges, Anoopshahur and Allyghur. Letters of light weight were managed to be conveyed with tolerable safety by that route, notwithstanding that large sums were offered for the murder of those caught in the act of conveying English correspondence.

8. On or about the 5th June the troops at Allahabad, Cawnpore, Futtehgurh, Hameerpore, Banda Jansie, Lullutpore and Saugor mutinied; and, in consequence, all the post offices and mail lines in the Doab and Bundlekund as low down as Mirzapore became disorganized. Communication between Agra, the Cis-Sutledge States and Calcutta was then fairly cut off and could not be re-established by the Grand Trunk Road so long as Delhi remained in the possession of the mutineers. The route via Multan to Bombay was, however, open and instructions were given for the mails to and from the N.-W.P., Cis-Sutledge and Punjab being forwarded via Lahore.

9. Between Agra and Bombay the mail was not interrupted till the mutiny of the Gwalior Contingent on the 17th June, and since

then up to 1st February, 1858, or a period of seven months and thirteen days, the road via Gwalior and Indore to Bombay was closed or not practicable and safe for the mail.

10. So soon as it was apparent that the mail between Bombay and Agra could not be re-established via Gwalior and Indore, the establishment of runners between Agra, Jeypore, Naseerabad, Deesa and Ahmedabad was strengthened, and the mails to and from Bombay, Calcutta, Madras, etc., were very regularly conveyed by that route.

11. In the course of the month of August, Dr. Clark managed at Agra to organize an establishment of kossids, thence via Etawah to Cawnpore, and for very light letters not exceeding a ¼ tola in weight the arrangements, although occasionally interrupted, were generally successful excepting for a period of nearly eighteen days in the end of November and beginning of December, when the troops of the Gwalior Contingent crossed the Jumna and invested Cawnpore. On the defeat of the Gwalior Contingent at Cawnpore on the 7th December the kossid dak was again useful in keeping up communication between Agra and Cawnpore until the 5th January, 1858, when the mail carts were re-established after having ceased to run from the 5th June, or a period of seven months.

12. Communication with the province of Kemaon was uninterruptedly maintained by an establishment of runners posted via Sreenugger, Teeree, Mussoorie and Deyrah Dhoon.

13. Between Meerut and the Camp at Delhi runners were posted via Bagput, but they were frequently cut off, and the communication had to be kept up via Shamlie and Kurnaul or via Seharunpore and Umballa. When the runners between Meerut and the Camp at Delhi were intercepted it was frequently impossible to open direct communication even by kossids, so closely was the country infested with insurgents.

14. The mail cart establishment between the Camp at Delhi and Lahore was steadily kept up. Occasionally it was unsafe to take the carts over the twelve miles leading to and from the Camp,

and there the coachman rode the horses across country or proceeded on foot and so managed to elude the insurgents.

15. The mail cart establishment was the only available means by which officers could travel to and from the Camp before Delhi, and it afforded them an easy and speedy mode of travelling.

16. Extra horses were posted at each stage between the Jhellum and Delhi to admit of express cart daks being laid when necessary for mails or passengers.

17. In the month of August it became necessary to provide means for the removal of the sick and wounded officers from the Camp in Delhi to Kurnaul or Umballa, and some of the Inland Transit Company's carriages, in addition to the palanquin carriages and vans attached to the Post Office, were hired for the purpose. All sick and wounded officers were allowed, at the recommendation of the Brigadier-General, now Sir Archdale Wilson, to travel free of expense. Many valuable lives were thus saved.

18. I consider the conduct of the native coachmen beyond all praise during the disturbances. Great temptations to desert us were held out to them by the mutineers, but not one of them proved unfaithful to Government. From the date of arrival of our troops before Delhi on the 8th June till the 20th of September, the date of the fall of Delhi, the coachmen conveyed the mails to and from the Camp with the same safety and the same regularity as before the outbreak.

19. The public mind of the Punjab and Cis-Sutledge States was at the highest pitch of excitement watching the result of the operations of our troops against the mutineers at Delhi, and any interruption of the mail would have had a fatal effect on the peace of those States. The telegraph wire connecting the Camp with the Punjab was frequently cut, and thus it may be easily understood that the regularity of the mail throughout the crisis was of the most vital importance.

20. The Commissioner of Scinde, anticipating the possibility of the communication between the Punjab and Scinde or Bombay

being cut off, organized on his own responsibility a mail establishment between Bhawulpore and Jaudhpore, and again with Deesa and Hyderabad. This arrangement was useful in conveying intelligence between Agra, the Punjab and Central India, and also as an auxiliary line of communication between the Punjab and Bombay.

21. In the middle and end of July the mail cart establishment between Googairah and Mooltan became very clamorous and appeared to be inclined to strike. The vital importance of that establishment made me determine on travelling to Mooltan so as to ascertain whether the contractors had any reasonable grievance. There had been many expresses besides passenger daks, and their horses had been perhaps somewhat overworked in consequence, and accordingly I authorized an additional horse at each stage, which for the time quieted the contractors and they gave no more trouble. I was not without some suspicion that there were political influences exciting dissatisfaction amongst them. This impression was in some degree corroborated by an effort on the part of the prisoners of the jail at Googairah attempting to effect their escape. Happily, through the prompt and rigorous measures adopted by the Deputy Commissioner, Mr. Elphinstone, the *émeute* amongst the prisoners was most successfully crushed and the peace of the district was not disturbed. Otherwise the mails would have there been interrupted.

22. On the 14th September insurrection broke out between Googairah and Hurruppa. Many horses of the mail cart establishment were carried off by the rebels. Several carts were burnt, and communication by the direct route between Lahore and Mooltan was for several days wholly cut off. The local authorities of the district had no warning of the outbreak till the morning of the night on which it took place. The District Officers gave me reason to hope that the insurrection would be instantly put down, but unfortunately, owing to their paucity of troops, the rebels were not overawed sufficiently to admit of the mails being conveyed by the direct road within fifteen days. In the interim,

however, they were, after several days' stoppage, conveyed via Shahpore and Seeah to and from Mooltan and Lahore.

23. It is here worthy of remark that the successful assault of Delhi on the 14th September by our troops was telegraphed to Lahore, and full particulars thereof were transmitted by the mail of that date from Lahore to Mooltan, Scinde, Bombay, etc., before the outbreak between Googairah and Humppa. The receipt of the news of the successful assault of Delhi was signally opportune in Scinde, as the native troops then at Karachi, Hyderabad and Shikarpore were in a state approaching to open mutiny.

24. The route for the mail between Lahore and Mooltan via Shahpore being very circuitous and also unsafe as the country between the Sutledge and Ravee and even for some distance west of the Ravee was in open revolt, it became necessary to determine on having a more direct line of communication between Lahore, Scinde and Bombay. Accordingly a camel dak was established by the Chief Commissioner of the Punjab between Bhawulpore and Ferozepore. The head overseer of the Jullunder Division, Hurdeo Bux, was transferred for the superintendence of this dak and managed it most successfully.

25. The establishment of runners between Ferozepore, Lahore and Loodianah was at the same time strengthened in view to provide for the extra weight of the mails in transit via Bhawulpore, and thus the stations east and west of the Sutledge were rendered independent of the direct mail line between Lahore and Mooltan in respect to Scinde, Bombay, Calcutta, etc., etc.

26. The post offices and mail lines at and above Meerut and throughout the Cis-Sutledge States and Punjab have continued in uninterrupted operation excepting those situated on the line of road between Googairah and Humppa, which were for a short time the scene of insurrections in September.

APPENDIX H

THE WORK OF THE FIELD POST OFFICE BETWEEN 1867 AND 1912

The Abyssinian Expedition.

AT the end of September, 1867, the Postmaster-General, Bombay, reported that a reconnoitring party under Colonel Merewether, Political Agent, had left for Abyssinia and a Field Force was shortly to follow. A post office under Mr. J. Gardiner as Inspecting Postmaster sailed for Abyssinia on the 25th November along with the second detachment of the Expeditionary Force. A portion of the staff was left at Massowah, where the troops disembarked, and the rest was ordered to advance with the Army. Having fallen ill through overwork, Mr. Gardiner was replaced by Mr. E. de C. Williams on the 1st March, 1868.

Ordinary postage stamps were used, the denominations of the stamps supplied for the Field Force being ½ anna, 1 anna, 2 annas, 4 annas, 6 annas 8 pies, and 8 annas 8 pies. The postage payable on articles *for* members of the Expeditionary Force was as follows:

> LETTERS—4 annas for every ½ oz., 8 annas for 1 oz. and 8 annas for every additional oz. in excess of the first oz.
>
> NEWSPAPERS—8 pies for 4 ozs., 1 anna 4 pies for 8 ozs.
>
> BOOKS—2 annas for 4 ozs., 4 annas for 8 ozs. and 4 annas for every additional 8 ozs.

Prepayment in the latter two cases being compulsory. It does not appear that parcels or money orders were exchanged or Savings Bank transactions allowed.

The postal officials began to return from Abyssinia by the end of June, 1868, the last batch arriving at Bombay on the 4th July.

The Afghanistan Expedition.

The war broke out in November, 1878, and Mr. J. H. Cornwall was appointed to take charge of postal arrangements with the column under the command of General Stewart, Mr. W. T. van Someren with the column under the command of Major-General F. S. Roberts, and Mr. J. L. Fendal with the Peshawar column. The approximate strength of the whole force was about 45,000 fighting men and 60,000 camp followers. The mails between Quetta and Kandahar were conveyed under the control of the Political Agent and the military authorities.

When General Roberts moved out, a hill cart service was opened from Kohat to Thull, a distance of sixty-four miles, in the Kurram Valley. The principal difficulty was the work of organizing and maintaining the mail lines, which were also used for conveying military stores. Apart from the work done at the Post Office workshops at Aligarh, workshops had to be opened at Rawalpindi, Jund, Thull and other places for the construction and repair of carts. In this expedition non-commissioned officers were taught to do postal work, and whenever they were required to do so they were allowed a postal salary of Rs.30 a month.

The control of the whole postal arrangements devolved upon Colonel W. M. Lane, Postmaster-General, Punjab, and it was due to his exertions that the arrangements met with success.

Malta Expeditionary Force.

In April, 1878, it was decided to send an Expeditionary Force to Malta under Major-General J. Ross, C.B., and at the instance of the military authorities a small postal staff, consisting of a postmaster (Mr. Dinshaw Jijibhoy) with a clerk and three peons, was selected to accompany the troops. The postal arrangements were made under the direction of the Postmaster-General, Bombay, and the Expeditionary Force started from Bombay on the 1st May, 1878.

When the island of Cyprus was ceded to Great Britain by

Turkey the Indian Contingent went to occupy it, and the postal staff was accordingly ordered to embark for Cyprus. A British post office was opened at Larnaka and Mr. Dinshaw was placed in charge of it, and there he worked conjointly with the British postal staff till his return to India on the 22nd August, 1878. Shortly after Sir Garnet Wolseley came out from England as Governor, and the island was then divided into six parts, each with a Civil Commissioner and garrisoned by a regiment. The Commissioners were ex-officio postmasters of their respective divisions, and there was no regular arrangement between these divisions for the exchange of mails, which were occasionally conveyed by means of Japties or policemen. When Cyprus was first occupied there was only a fortnightly communication with India by means of the Austrian Lloyd Steam Navigation Company's steamers; subsequently a weekly service was also established by the Bells Asia Minor Line of steamers. A small Austrian post office at Larnaka was permitted, and this served the entire island.

The field post office was opened at Malta on the 27th May and closed at Cyprus on the 22nd August, 1878.

Egypt Expeditionary Force.

In the beginning of July, 1882, the Government of India directed an Expeditionary Force of about 7000 men of all arms for service in Egypt under the command of Major-General Sir H. Macpherson, V.C., K.C.B.

The postal arrangements were made by Mr. Fanshawe, Post-master-General, Bombay, and Mr. J. H. Cornwall, who had special experience of the management of field post offices in Afghanistan, was selected as the Chief Superintendent of Field Post Offices.

The Indian field post office establishment started from Bombay on the 22nd August, 1882, and returned there on the 31st October of the same year.

Kalahandi Expedition.

The rising of Khonds in Kalahandi, an important feudatory State in the Chattisgarh Division in Central Provinces, necessitated the despatch of troops. In June, 1882, the Deputy Postmaster-General, Central Provinces, reported that the rising was of a serious character and that the country was not likely to be quiet for some time. The troops marched from Sambalpur and Raipur, and three field post offices were opened to serve them.

Mr. P. Gorman, Superintendent of the Division, was in entire charge of the postal arrangements. The expedition lasted for only a short time, but the communications had to be maintained till about the end of the year.

Suakim Field Post Office, 1885.

In February, 1885, it was decided to send an Expeditionary Force composed of Indian troops to Egypt, and the Director-General was asked to make arrangements for a field post office to accompany it. Mr. O'Shea, as Chief Superintendent, was in charge of the postal staff, under the direction of the Postmaster-General, Bombay.

The strength of the Expeditionary Force was 10,517, including followers, and General Hudson, C.B., was in command of the force. The postal staff started from Bombay on the afternoon of the 24th February, 1885, and on the 7th March, 1885, arrived at Suakim, where the Base post office was opened on the 8th current. Mails were exchanged between Egypt and India by Government transports and P. & O. packets. Only two officers, Messrs. O'Shea and Lalkaka, received medals, and none were granted to the subordinate postal staff. The field post office was closed in November, 1885.

The Upper Burma Expedition.

On the 23rd October, 1885, the Government of India asked the Director-General to make the postal arrangements for the Expeditionary Force in Upper Burma. The strength of the Force consisted of 10,000 fighting men and 2000 followers, besides 1000 dhooly bearers and 3000 coolies. On the 10th November, 1885, the Expedition, under the command of Major-General H. N. D.

Prendergast, C.B., V.C., left Rangoon for Upper Burma by steamers up the Irrawaddy river to Thayetmyo and thence by the land route to Mandalay. Mr. G. Barton Groves, Deputy Postmaster-General, Burma, was called on to organize the service and accompany the Force as Deputy Postmaster-General in charge. The Rangoon, Prome and Thayetmyo post offices were strengthened, and the last-named was converted into a Base office. Five field post offices were also opened on board the head-quarters steamers of each of the five brigades which composed the force.

The Pishin Field Force.

In March, 1885, the Governor-General in Council decided to increase the garrison in Baluchistan to a strength of three divisions comprising about 25,000 men and 20,000 followers, and the necessary postal arrangements had to be made. Mr. J. Short, Deputy Postmaster-General, Sind and Baluchistan, was in charge, assisted by Mr. E. Walker, Inspector of post offices.

In April, 1885, a head office was opened at Rindli, in Baluchistan, which was designated the " Pishin Force Frontier Office," and the Quetta post office was strengthened. Nine camp post offices were also opened, and mails were carried to these offices by camels and sowars.

Sikkim Expedition.

The orders for the despatch of a force for operations in Sikkim were notified in the *Gazette of India* of the 3rd March, 1888. Shortly after the commencement of hostilities the Government of Bengal requested Mr. H. M. Kisch, Postmaster-General, Bengal, to open a runners' line from Siliguri to Kalimpong, a distance of thirty-seven miles. This line was used only for transmission of letter mails, parcel mails being conveyed by the old route from Darjeeling via Ghum and Pasok. On the 24th March the Padong post office was converted into a sub-office, and from that date it was constituted a Base office for the expedition.

On the 16th March the force, which concentrated at Padong, moved out in two columns, one under Brigadier-General T.

Graham, R.A., commanding the expedition, and the other under Colonel Michel, of the 13th Bengal Infantry, the former advancing towards Fort Lingtu and the other towards the Rhenok Bazar. With the advance of troops the post office opened at Dulapchin was shortly removed to Ranglichu. Other post offices were opened at Gnatong, Sedonchin, Gangtok, Rhenok Bazar and Pakyong. The mail lines connecting these offices were under the management of the Post Office as far as Ronglichu and Pakyong, but the lines beyond were under the Political authorities.

The Black Mountain or Hazara Field Force.

Towards the beginning of September, 1888, the Home Government having decided to send a punitive expedition against the tribesmen of the Black Mountain, a Field Force was organized on the Hazara frontier. The object of the expedition was to punish the Khan Khel Hassanzai and the Akazai tribes. Brigadier-General J. W. McQueen, C.B., Commanding the Punjab Frontier Force, directed the expedition. On the 8th September, 1888, Mr. W. T. van Someren, Superintendent of post offices, Rawalpindi Division, was deputed to make the postal arrangements with the force. Haripur was constituted a Base office for the Derband column, and Abbottabad for the Oghi column. The tonga service from Hassan Abdal to Abbottabad was strengthened and extended to Mansera, and a mixed tonga and horse service was established between Abbottabad and Oghi. A runners' line was opened from Haripur to Derband. A railway sorting office, under the supervision of Mr. N. G. Wait, was also opened at Hassan Abdal for the sorting and onward transmission of articles for the Field Force.

The Chin Expedition, Burma.

In December, 1888, a small force of about 1200 men, besides civil officers and followers, headed by Brigadier-General Faunce, started for the Chindwin Division to quell a rising of Burmans and to reduce to order the country which was then infested with dacoits. The expedition was undertaken very suddenly, and the

Quartermaster-General in India asked the Deputy Postmaster-General, Burma, to arrange for the opening of a field post office at Kalemyo at a distance of twenty-seven miles from the base of operations at Kalewa. About July, 1889, the country was brought to a normal state and the troops were withdrawn.

The Lushai Expedition.

In 1888 the Government of India having decided to send a punitive expedition against the Shendus and other tribes in the Chitagong Hill Tracts, a small force under Colonel V. W. Tregear was organized and concentrated at Demagiri. The force was styled the "Lushai Expeditionary Force," and consisted of about 1200 men besides followers and coolies. An inspector was deputed to make the postal arrangements. The boat line from Rangamati to Demagiri, which was maintained by the Frontier Police, was strengthened, also the post offices at Rangamati and Demagiri, the latter being constituted a base office, and a post office was opened at Barkul—half-way between Rangamati and Demagiri—where there was a stockade of military police. The troops kept the field for about four months and came back at the end of April, 1889.

The Chin Lushai Expedition.

In 1889 two armies operated in this expedition, one from Burma and the other from Chittagong. The troops in Burma were divided into two columns, one operating from Fort White as a base against the Syins and other tribes, and the other starting from Gangaw as a base and advancing via Yokwa on Haka. The Chittagong force advanced from Fort Lungleh on Haka. Brigadier-General W. P. Symons commanded the operations on the Burma side, and Colonel Tregear commanded the Chittagong column. The strength of the force concentrated at Gangaw consisted of about 40 officers, 1200 European and Indian troops and 2500 followers. The strength of the Chittagong column consisted of about 3500 men besides followers and coolies.

On the Burma side much difficulty was experienced by the

supervising officers in organizing and maintaining the lines, which lay over sandy beds of rivers, hillocks and jungles and on the Chittagong side, on account of constant illness and the consequent change of officials deputed. Mr. J. W. McCrea, Superintendent of post offices, Burma Circle, was deputed to make postal arrangements for the force under the direction of Mr. G. J. Hynes, Deputy Postmaster-General, Burma. On the other side postal arrangements were made by Mr. G. S. Clifford, Superintendent of post offices, under the direction of Mr. G. Barton Groves, Deputy Postmaster-General, Eastern Bengal.

The Zhob Expedition.

The object of the expedition was to explore the borders of the Zhob Valley and to take steps either to capture the outlaw Dost Muhammad or to expel him from the Kakar country and to coerce the Khiddarzai Shirani tribe into submission.

Towards the middle of September, 1890, intimation was received from the Quartermaster-General in India that a force of about 2000 men, besides camp followers, was about to start for the Zhob Valley, and on the 27th of that month a small field post office, consisting of a sub-postmaster and two peons, started from Quetta with a portion of the troops for Hindubagh, which was to be the general rendezvous. The expedition was commanded by Sir George White.

The Black Mountain Expedition.

In 1891 a force was sent for operations against the Hassanzai and Akazai tribes of the Black Mountains. The strength of the force, which was under the command of Major-General Elles, C.B., was about 6800 men, and it advanced from Darband in two columns—one marching via Baradar and Pailam to Tilli, and the other along the river route via Kotkai and Kunhar. The postal arrangements were made by Mr. W. T. van Someren under the direction of Mr. G. J. Hynes, Postmaster-General, Punjab.

The Chin Hills Expedition.

The Government of India sanctioned military operations in the north and east frontier of the Bhamo district and Chin Hills during the cold season of 1891–92. In the Bhamo direction the object of the expedition was to explore the amber and jade mines, the Hukong Valley and the country on the east and north-east frontier above the Taeping river on the Chinese border. The expedition had a quasi-military character, and about 5000 troops, including police battalions, operated in various columns, under the direction of Major-General R. C. Stewart, commanding the Burma districts.

Mr. F. McCrea, Inspector of post offices, Eastern Division, was deputed to organize and supervise the arrangements.

The Manipur Expedition.

The outbreak in Manipur in 1891, and the consequent massacre of Mr. Quinton, the Chief Commissioner of Assam, and his party, necessitated the despatch of troops to quell the rebellion. The force was designated the "Manipur Field Force," and about 2500 men, including followers, operated from the Tammu side and about the same number from Kohima and Silchar. Mr. W. Roussac was in charge of the postal arrangements with the Tammu column, and Mr. F. P. Williams, assisted by an inspector, with the Kohima column. All correspondence for the Tammu column was sent from India to Rangoon and thence by boats to Kindat. From Kindat to Tammu the mails were conveyed by runners, and a runners' line was opened from Tammu to Manipur. These arrangements worked for a very short time on account of the rapid advance of troops and their immediate return.

The Miranzai Expedition.

The object of the expedition, which was under the command of Brigadier-General Sir William Lockhart, K.C.B., was to overawe the recalcitrant Samil clans of the Urakzai tribe in the

Miranzai Valley. The force was ordered to the front in January, 1891, and advanced in three columns, the first column having its base at Shahu Khel, the second at Tog and the third at Hangu. Mr. A. Bean, Superintendent of post offices, Peshawar Division, was placed in charge of field postal arrangements connected with the force in addition to his own duties.

The Wuntho Expedition.

On the 15th February, 1891, the station of Kawlin was suddenly attacked by a party of rebels from the Wuntho State, in Upper Burma, and a few police who formed the garrison of the place had to evacuate it. The post office had to be abandoned and the sub-postmaster had to come away along with the other officials. A combined force of police and military, consisting of about 2500 men, was at once organized and advanced on Wuntho from Shwebo, Katha and Tigyaing to put down the rebellion and bring the country under permanent occupation. The troops employed were not designated a Field Force, and the postal arrangements were therefore carried out on ordinary scale and not according to the rules of the Field Service Manual.

The Isazai Field Force.

In September, 1892, the Government of India decided to send out an expedition under Major-General Sir William Lockhart to punish certain villages of the trans-Indus Isazai clans who had harboured Hashim Ali Khan of Seri in contravention of their agreement entered into at Seri in May, 1891. A force of about 4000 men of all arms concentrated at Derband and was styled the "Isazai Field Force." On the 17th September, 1892, Mr. C. J. Dease, Superintendent of post offices, was deputed to make the special arrangements for the force with the assistance of an inspector.

Kurram Field Force.

In the beginning of October, 1892, the Government of India decided to depute a Political officer at the head of a force in the

Lower Kurram Valley. The object was to expel the Chikkai tribes from the valley and to effect a thorough settlement of the country. The force which accompanied the Political officer, Mr. W. R. H. Merk, C.S.I., consisted of about 2500 men, including followers. Mr. P. Sheridan, Postmaster-General, Punjab, arranged for field post offices, and the Superintendent of post offices, Peshawar Division, was placed in charge. By the end of October the presence of troops in Kurram was no longer necessary, and the field offices were closed with the exception of the head-quarters office, which was retained for the use of the garrison.

The Wano Expedition.

In August, 1892, owing to disturbances in Afghanistan, a detachment of troops had to be sent beyond the frontier to take up position at Kajuri Kuch in the Wano country, thirty miles beyond the Gomal Pass. As there was no post office at the place, arrangements were made by the Superintendent of post offices, Derajat Division, to send and receive mails via Gomal post office. In September, however, owing to the despatch of further troops, the Post Office was called upon to make arrangements. By the end of April, 1893, the strength of the Kajuri and Jandola forces was considerably reduced, and the postal establishments were gradually abolished.

The Abor Expedition, 1894.

The only postal arrangements made in connection with this expedition, which lasted for a very short time, were the opening of a runners' line from Sadiya to Bomjur and the strengthening of the delivery staff of Sadiya post office by an additional postman.

The Waziristan Field Force.

In August, 1894, the Government of India sanctioned the despatch of troops to accompany the British Commissioner in connection with the Afghan boundary demarkation. Pundit Shiv Pal, the Superintendent of post offices, Derajat Division, was placed in charge assisted by two inspectors, till he was relieved by

Mr. W. T. van Someren, who was placed on special duty in this connection. The post office at Tank was temporarily converted into a Base head office, and three field post offices were opened to move with the force.

On the 3rd November the Mushud Waziri made a determined night attack on the British camp at Wano, and, although the attack was repulsed, it resulted in 120 casualties. In the beginning of December, 1894, the Government of India having sanctioned active operations in Waziristan, Lieutenant-General Sir William Lockhart, who was now placed in command, asked for an additional Superintendent, and Mr. A. Franks Ryan was placed on special duty with the force.

The Chitral Relief Force.

In the middle of March, 1895, a scheme was prepared for field operations in Chitral, the object of which was to compel Umra Khan of Jandol to withdraw from the Chitral country, and the Director-General was requested to make postal arrangements for the force, which consisted of about 20,000 troops of all arms and about 30,000 camp followers. This was the largest force mobilized in India since the Afghan War of 1879, and the postal arrangements had therefore to be made on a proportionately large scale. The expedition was titled "The Chitral Relief Force" and was commanded by Major-General Sir Robert Low, K.C.B.

On the 18th March, 1895, Mr. P. Sheridan, Postmaster-General, Punjab, was requested by the Director-General to arrange field post offices, and by the end of the month the postal staff, who were collected at Nowshera, were in readiness to start. Mr. A. Franks Ryan was the senior Superintendent in charge. In the early stages of the campaign considerable difficulty was experienced by the supervising officers in organizing lines for the conveyance of mails. Mule transport being very limited, pack bullocks had to be used for the first few days, and when those were withdrawn a temporary runners' line had to be opened. Information, however, was shortly received that the country was open as far as Durgai, a distance of forty-one miles from Nowshera, and arrangements were made with Messrs. Dhanjibhoy to open a tonga line.

On the 30th March the force moved out to Mardan and the head-quarters field post office went with it. On the 22nd April, 1895, information was received that Colonel Kelly had succeeded in reducing the Chitral fort from the Gilgit side, and a further hasty advance of troops was therefore no longer necessary. With the occupation of the Chitral territory by the 3rd Brigade the expedition practically came to an end. The Abbottabad Force was broken up on the 31st May, 1895.

Suakim Expedition, 1896.

In May, 1896, under orders from the Home Government, an Expeditionary Force, 3000 strong, was sent to Suakim under the command of Brigadier-General C. C. Egerton, C.B., D.S.O., and a field post office was ordered to accompany it. The chief of the postal staff was Mr. Bennett, who, however, did not hold the rank of Chief Superintendent as the Force was too small. It started on the 22nd May, 1896, and arrived on the 1st June at Suakim, where the Base office was opened. Subsequently a sub-office was opened at Tokar, and the exchange of mails between this office and the Base office was carried on by camel dak twice a week. There was fortnightly communication between India and Suakim by Egyptian steamers, and parcel and letter mails were conveyed by these and by P. & O. steamers. The field post office was closed on the 8th December, 1896.

The Malakand Field Force.

On the 31st July, 1897, the Adjutant-General in India forwarded to the Director-General a scheme for operations in the Malakand country, and Mr. P. Sheridan, Postmaster-General, Punjab and N.W.F., was requested to make special postal arrangements for the force. Mr. H. C. Sheridan, Assistant Director-General of the Post Office, was placed in charge.

By the middle of August all the troops forming the 1st and 2nd Brigades went across the Malakand to the Swat Valley. In the meantime, fresh trouble having arisen round and about Peshawar, the Government of India issued orders for punitive operations against the Mohmands, who had invaded British territory and attacked the village and fort of Shabkadar, nineteen miles from Peshawar. Accordingly a strong force was concentrated about the place, and Mr. C. A. Stowell was deputed to Peshawar to make special postal arrangements for this force. "The Mohmand Field Force," under Major-General Ellis, left Shabkadar on the 15th September and returned to Peshawar on the 8th October, 1897. During the expedition a small force was sent to Abazai to guard the works of the Swat Canal, and a field post office accompanied it.

On New Year's day of 1898 orders were issued for an advance to Buner, and the 2nd Brigade marched to Katlang, which was at once connected with Mardan by an ekka service, later extended to Sanghao. There were now two ekka services—one from Mardan to Rustam, a distance of nineteen miles, and the other from Mardan to Sanghao, a distance of twenty-one miles. On the 9th January the name of the force was changed to the "Buner Field Force." The postal arrangements for this force, which was not in existence for more than a fortnight, were in the hands of Mr. N. M. Cama, Superintendent of post offices.

The Malakand Field Force began to be demobilized on the 22nd January, 1898, but only a small portion of the troops returned to India. The rest went forward and became part of the Swat garrison. In this expedition arrangements were made for the first time for the sale of newspapers by field post offices, a service which was greatly appreciated. So efficient were the postal arrangements and the regularity of the tonga service that the mails to and from the front travelled with a punctuality which would compare favourably with any long-established line in India.

The Tirah Expedition.

On the 17th September, 1897, the Director-General was asked to make arrangements for a postal service for the Expeditionary Force to be sent against the Afridi and Orakzai tribes on the Kohat and Peshawar frontier. The Postmaster-General, Punjab and N.-W.F., Mr. P. Sheridan, was immediately communicated with, and Mr. van Someren was appointed Chief Postal Superintendent with the expedition.

The Base post office for the main force was at first situated at Kohat, and the Base office for the Peshawar column at Peshawar. When the troops marched through Tirah and took up their position for the winter in the Bara Valley, the Khyber Pass and the neighbourhood of Peshawar, Messrs. Dhanjibhoy established two tonga services connecting Peshawar with Bara and Jamrud, while beyond these places they arranged for the carriage of mails by a horse post. The mail service for the Peshawar column previous to this had been carried on by the Afridi horse contractors, and as the roads were improved the tonga services were extended up to Landi Kotal in the Khyber Pass and Gandao in the Bara Valley.

The postal arrangements lasted for a period of six months. On this occasion, too, the field post offices were specially authorized to sell newspapers to the troops and were allowed a commission on the sales.

The Tochi Field Force.

The postal arrangements in connection with the Tochi Field Force lasted for a period of about eight months, from July, 1897, to February, 1898.

The base of the operations was Bannu, which is 111 miles away from the railway at Khushalgarh, and, as soon as it was known that a force was to be mobilized at Bannu, arrangements were made for the introduction of an efficient tonga service from Khushalgarh to that place and for a proper railway connection between Golra and Khushalgarh. Between Khushalgarh and Kohat a feeble tonga service was already in existence under the management of the District Board of Kohat, while for the local demands an ekka service had been established between Kohat and Bannu. Neither of these lines could be relied upon to meet the special requirements for mails and passengers caused by the expedition, and Mr. Dhanjibhoy, the mail contractor of the Rawalpindi–Srinagar line, established a complete and efficient tonga service over the entire distance.

The postal arrangements were carried out very satisfactorily. Mr. W. T. van Someren was in charge of the actual arrangements in the field from the beginning till September, 1897, when he was relieved by Mr. F. O'Byrne, who remained in charge during the remainder of the operations.

The Tochi Valley Field Force.

After the breaking up of the Tochi Field Force in December, 1897, it was decided to retain in the valley a brigade of troops on field service scale under the command of the General Officer Commanding, Tochi. The troops were quartered in six military posts, and camp post offices were opened to serve them. During the Tochi Expedition there was a tonga service between Edwardesabad and Bannu, but this having been discontinued a new arrangement had to be made for a tonga service with Messrs. Dhanjibhoy and Sons for the conveyance of mails between Khushalgarh and Kohat and an ekka service between Edwardesabad and Miranshah and Datta Khel.

The Swat Valley Column.

When the second division of the Tirah Force was demobilized it was decided to retain a strong column in the Swat Valley to take up positions in Dir territory for the protection of the line of communications and the route of the relieving and relieved Chitral Force. The arrangement necessitated the opening of three field post offices from the 1st May, 1898, and from the same date the Swat Sorting Office at Nowshera was strengthened. It was also decided to retain the services of a Superintendent to accompany the column up to Dir territory and return with the relieved troops from Chitral.

The postal arrangements had to be maintained till the end of June, when the column having been considerably reduced, two field offices were abolished and only one was retained till the 15th July, 1898.

The Mishmi Expedition.

In November, 1899, the Director-General was requested to open a field branch post office at Bonjur and connect it by a runners' line (twenty-four miles long) with Sadiya, where there was a civil post office. This place was made the base of operations of the Mishmi Field Force. About 200 military police and 1000 regular troops operated in this expedition, which began in December, 1899, and ended in January, 1900. The Bonjur office was opened on the 1st December, 1899, and closed on the 9th February, 1900.

The China Expeditionary Force.

At the request of the Home Government, a force entitled "The China Expeditionary Force" was mobilized in India for service in China under the command of General Sir A. Gaselee. The first intimation of the despatch of the army was received on the 29th June, 1900. This, however, referred only to one brigade of troops of all arms; but on the 25th June intimation was received that a force of two brigades with divisional troops were under orders for China. The control of the field postal arrangements was in the hands of Mr. Stewart-Wilson, Postmaster-General, Punjab, under whose orders the postal staff was mobilized and equipped. At first it was decided to fit out twelve field post offices to accompany the force. Mr. W. T. van Someren was appointed Chief Superintendent, and Mr. A. Bean and Mr. A. B. Thompson were selected to work under him.

By the end of August, 1900, the force in China was strengthened by a cavalry brigade, one infantry brigade and three large coolie corps, and the postal staff had to be supplemented. Thus by the end of the year there were in China :

1 Chief Superintendent.
4 Superintendents.
4 Inspectors.
1 Postmaster.
2 Deputy Postmasters.
20 Sub-Postmasters.
53 Clerks.
76 Followers.

On the 29th June, 1900, a notification was issued regarding the conditions under which postal articles could be exchanged with the China Expeditionary Force. The Indian Base office was at first opened at Linkung-tao (Wei Hai Wei), but was shortly transferred to Hongkong. Articles for the force were despatched by the steamers of the B.I.S.N. Company, the Messageries Maritimes and also by the Opium steamers to Hongkong. The Colonial post office at Hongkong had an arrangement with all merchant vessels binding them to carry mails as far as Shanghai, and owing to the courtesy of the Postmaster-General, Hongkong, this concession was made use of to carry the mails of the Field Force. North of Shanghai the mails were carried by transports and men-o'-war. Later on the Chinese Imperial Postal Authorities carried our mails from Shanghai to Taku and back free of charge until the latter port was closed by the winter ice. Another route had then to be chosen for the North China mails, and once more we had to resort to the kindness of the Imperial Chinese Post Office, who agreed to supply transport from Chifu to Chaingwantao twice a week on condition that half the cost of the coal used should be paid. Thus the mails were conveyed from Hongkong to Shanghai, from Shanghai to Chifu and from Chifu to Chaingwantao and thence to Tientsin. The chief postal land routes were (1) Taku to Pekin and (2) Tientsin to Shanhaikwan.

Dollar currency was used in the field offices, the rate of a dollar being fixed at 1s. 11d., equivalent to Rs.1.7.0. The first postal detachment took with them a full supply of postage stamps, post-cards, etc., but it was found inadvisable to use them owing to the fact that it would be impossible to sell them at a price exactly equivalent to face value. At Hongkong the postal equivalent for 10 centimes, i.e. 1 anna, is 4 cents. It followed, therefore, that twenty-five 1-anna stamps could be bought for a dollar and that the purchaser would be able to make 2 annas for every dollar spent on stamps, and it was feared that advantage would be taken of this to buy up Indian stamps wholesale for remittance to India. The postage stamps were therefore overprinted with the letters "C.E.F.," i.e. "China Expeditionary Force, so that their use would be localized, and the surcharged stamps came into circulation about the middle of August, 1900. In order to confine the use of field offices to the members of the force, orders were issued that our postage stamps should not be sold except to soldiers and officers in uniform. The rates of postage fixed for all purposes were those in force in India, the postage to India being reckoned at Indian inland rates.

Difficulty had all along been felt in supplying postal facilities to the small bodies of troops stationed at or near railway stations where there were no post offices. Mr. van Someren removed this difficulty by introducing a combined Post and Railway Mail Service between Pekin and Taku and Tientsin and Shanhaikwan, a scheme which was a new one in the history of the field postal service. Postal clerks had not only to sort letters in the trains, but also to receive and deliver letters and sell postage stamps at each railway station. By August, 1901, there was a reduction of the number of troops in China and fourteen field post offices were closed, the supervising staff being reduced to a Chief Superintendent and an inspecting postmaster in North China and a Superintendent and an inspecting postmaster at Hongkong. Mr. van Someren left China on the 5th August, 1901, leaving Mr. Thompson in charge.

This was the first occasion that a large postal establishment had to be sent out with a military expedition overseas to a foreign country. The force consisted of over 37,000 men stationed at various places from Shanghai to Taku and Taku to Pekin. The harmonious relations with the Chinese Imperial Postal Administration and the material assistance which it rendered on every possible occasion greatly helped to the success of the Indian Field Post Office administration in China.

The Somaliland Field Force.

The postal arrangements made to serve the Somaliland Field Force extended over a period of nearly two years from January, 1903, to November, 1904. Mr. Wynch, who was appointed Chief Superintendent, remained till June, 1904, when he was invalided and relieved by Mr. A. J. Hughes, who held charge until the end of the operations. The strength of the force was 3000, and at first one base office and one field post office, with one postmaster, five clerks and four packers, were provided. Mails were exchanged between India and Somaliland by Government transports. The field post offices were closed on the 25th November, 1904.

The Tibet Mission.

In 1903 the Government of India decided to send a small force to escort the Tibet Frontier Commission. At first a number of temporary post offices and lines were opened under the control of the Superintendent of post offices, Jalpaiguri Division, to serve the Mission, but it was not until it was decided that the Mission should advance into the Chumbi Valley that field post offices and lines were required. The Mission was headed by Colonel Younghusband and the escort was commanded by General MacDonald, with Mr. H. Tulloch as Chief Superintendent.

The rapid development of field post offices necessitated the appointment of a second Superintendent, and Mr. A. Bean was deputed to field service. On the 6th January, 1904, Mr. Bean took over charge of the Base Division, but shortly after died of heart disease on the 3rd March, 1904. The entire arrangements then devolved again on Mr. Tulloch until the 1st April, 1904, when Mr. C. J. Dease took over charge of the Base Division.

The Mission advanced on Gyantse on the 4th April. From Tuna to Gyantse the mail arrangements were in the hands of the military authorities, and only one postal clerk, whose duty it was to distribute letters, was sent up with the escort. The Mission reached Gyantse on the 14th May, and a field post office had to be opened there and at several other places on the lines of communications. The force remained at Lhassa from the 3rd August to the 23rd September and returned to Gyantse on the 6th October, 1904. There was by this time at Gyantse an accumulation of over 1100 parcels addressed to the members of the Lhassa column, but Mr. Angelo, who was then placed in charge of the advance division, disposed of them in three days before the troops left on their return march. The demobilization of the force began by the end of October, and the postal officials were ordered to leave Chumbi on the 26th and to close the field post offices between Chumbi and Gangtok on their way down. Mr. Tulloch relinquished charge of the F.P.O.'s on the 28th November, 1904.

The Bazar Valley Field Force.

The postal arrangements made to serve the Bazar Valley Field Force extended over a period of twenty-five days, from the 13th February to the 8th March, 1908. On the night of the 12th February the Chief of the Staff informed the Postmaster, Peshawar, that the force would leave the station the next morning. A base office, four first-class field post offices and three second-class field post offices were sent to the front, and on receipt of the scheme for the organization and mobilization of the force on the 14th February this establishment was reduced considerably. The work of the field post offices on this occasion was limited almost entirely to the disposal of articles of the letter and packet mails.

The Mohmand Field Force.

The postal arrangements made to serve the Mohmand Field Force extended over a period of thirty-eight days, from the 28th April to the 4th June, 1908. The first intimation that an expedition would take place was received on the 23rd April, and the Postmaster-General, Punjab and N.-W.F., was at once directed to make all arrangements to serve the troops that were concentrating on the frontier. Mr. McMinn, who was Chief Superintendent of post offices with the Bazar Valley Field Force, was placed in charge.

The Abor Expeditionary Force, 1911–12.

The postal arrangements made to serve the Abor Expeditionary Force extended over a period of about one year, from May, 1911, to May, 1912. A temporary post office was first opened on the 15th May, 1911, at Saikwaghat, a terminus of the Dibru–Sadiyah Railway, to serve the troops making preparations there for the expedition. The office was under the control of the Superintendent of post offices, Upper Assam Division. It was not until September, 1911, when the force advanced towards Kobo, that the Department was called upon to organize a field postal service. The arrangements were placed under the control of the Postmaster-General, Eastern Bengal and Assam, and for the supervision of the work in the field Mr. A. J. Faichnie, Superintendent of post offices, Upper Assam Division, was, in addition to his own duties, appointed Superintendent of Field Post Offices, assisted by an inspector.

APPENDIX J

THE POST OFFICE INSURANCE FUND

THE suggestion to establish a State Life Assurance was first made in 1872 by Sir Richard Temple, the Finance Member of Council. After a great deal of discussion it was dropped in 1873, but was revived again in 1881 by Mr. Hogg, the Director-General of the Post Office, when it was accepted by the Viceroy's Council and finally by the Secretary of State.

The principal features of the scheme which was actually introduced on the 1st February, 1884, were:

(1) For the time the Fund was confined to the employés of the Post Office.

(2) Provision was made for effecting life insurance in three ways, viz.—

- (i) By a single payment.
- (ii) By monthly payments until the person insured attained the age of 50 or 55.
- (iii) By monthly payments during life.

(3) Provision was also made for two classes of monthly allowances, viz. "Immediate" or "Deferred."

(4) One life could be insured for any sum which was a multiple of Rs.50 up to the total of Rs.4,000, and the monthly allowance granted on any one life might consist of any sum which was a multiple of Rs.8 up to the limit of Rs.50.

(5) Medical examination of proposers for insurance was made free.

(6) Arrangements were made for the deduction of the monthly premia from the insured person's salary except the first premium or premium paid during leave without pay.

(7) Policies and contracts issued under the scheme were exempt from stamp duty.

The scheme worked smoothly, and, taking into consideration that many employés of the Post Office are poorly paid officials, a fair measure of success was attained during the first few years except in the Monthly Allowance branch and in the system of Life Insurance by single payment. The following figures show the proportion of officials who availed themselves of insurance during the first three years :—

1884–85 . .	1·05% of the whole Post Office establishment.			
1885–86 . .	1·46%	„	„	„
1886–87 . .	1·79%	„	„	„

In 1887 the rule under which one-half surrender value could be allowed on all policies and contracts when payment had been discontinued was modified so as to exclude from this privilege policies and contracts on which three years' premia or subscriptions had not been paid. In September, 1887, the Fund was opened to the Telegraph Department, and in 1895 to employés of the Indo-European Telegraphs and to women employed in all the departments.

With effect from the 1st February, 1898, the benefits of the scheme were extended generally to all permanent Government servants whose pay was audited in Civil or Public Works Account offices and all members of establishments of the Military Department, under audit of the Military Account offices, who were subject to Civil rules. From the same date a system of Endowment Assurances providing for payment at any age between 45 and 55 was introduced. With this general extension of the scheme it was decided that the medical examination of proposers for insurance should be more stringent and that medical officers, who had until then been examining proposers for insurance free of any charge, should be allowed a fee of Rs.4 for each examination, as their insurance work would be substantially increased. In the same year (1898) the system of Life Insurance by a single payment which had proved to be a failure, was abolished.

In 1899, Temporary Engineers and Temporary Upper Subordinates of the Public Works Department were allowed by Government to be admissible to the benefits of the Fund, provided that the Chief Engineer declared that they were eligible for admission. In 1903 it was extended to permanent Government servants in foreign service in India, and in the same year Life Insurance policies were allowed to be converted into Endowment Assurance policies.

In 1904, the following relaxations of the rules were sanctioned with a view to meet the convenience of Government servants.

(1) Insured persons who had retired from the service and whose pensions were paid in India were allowed the option of deducting their premia or subscriptions from their pension bills instead of being compelled to pay them in cash at a post office.

(2) When there was any difficulty in the way of a proposal being signed by the proposer in the presence of his immediate superior, this duty might, with the permission of the Postmaster-General, be performed in the presence of the local postmaster or any other responsible officer who had to sign the certificate.

(3) The table of subscriptions for "Immediate Monthly Allowance," which contained rates up to the age of sixty, was extended so as to provide for contracts with persons above that age.

In the same year the benefits of the Fund were extended to Temporary Lower Subordinates, clerks of the Public Works Department and to clerks of the Punjab University on the same conditions as to Temporary Engineers and Temporary Upper Subordinates.

The year 1907 witnessed several important changes in the Post Office Insurance Fund made on the recommendation of the Government Actuary. These were:

(1) That the sums eventually payable in respect of policies in existence on 31st March, 1907, in the Life Branch of the Fund were increased by 10 per cent and that the premia payable in respect of sums assured in that branch after that date would be correspondingly reduced. The rates of premia for Life Insurance were revised accordingly.

(2) That a life policy, with monthly payments payable till death, was allowed to be converted into a life policy with monthly payments payable to a specified age or into a fully paid up policy payable at death.

(3) That an endowment policy might be converted into a paid-up policy payable at some anterior date or at death, if earlier.

(4) That insurants could reduce their monthly premia to any desired extent from any specified date.

(5) That when a policy of either class was surrendered the policy holder should be given the full surrender value which on an actuarial calculation could be paid without loss to the Fund, instead of half that amount as hitherto given.

(6) That the surrender value of a lapsed policy was payable at any time after default, on application being made for the same.

(7) That the period up to which payment of arrears of premium or subscription was allowed for the revival of a policy of less than three years' duration was extended from three to six months.

The tables of premia, introduced at the time the Fund was started, as already stated, were calculated on the mortality rates which had been deduced from the experience of the Uncovenanted

Service Family Pension Fund, Bengal—a Fund which was confined to Europeans resident in India—there being no more reliable mortality statistics available for the purpose at the time. In 1909 the India Office Actuary, in his review on the operations of the Fund for the year 1907–08, noticed that, in view of the rapid growth of the scheme, it was necessary to revise the tables according to more accurate mortality statistics. In his review on the work of the Fund for 1908–09 the Actuary asked for detailed particulars of all the policies issued by the Fund since its institution in the form of statements, in order to enable him to deduce therefrom the necessary mortality rates, and thus prepare fresh tables of premia. These statistics were submitted with the Director-General's Annual Report on the operations of the Fund for the year 1910–11.

In the meantime it was brought to notice in 1909 that, under the existing method of calculating surrender values of Life policies, the values in certain cases were found on calculation to be considerably in excess of the total amount of premia paid on the policies. Taking advantage of this, insurants began to surrender their policies in large numbers. The matter was referred to the Secretary of State. As a result, the Actuary at the India Office forwarded revised tables for the calculation of surrender values of Life policies, to be used until the general revision of the Mortality tables and of the tables of premia, which had been under contemplation, was effected. In 1909 an important concession was sanctioned regarding the payment of premia by insured persons while on leave or suspension or when retiring. It was laid down that an insured person should not be considered as in arrears of premium or subscription for any month so long as he has not drawn any pay, pension or suspension allowance.

In 1910, with a view to afford greater facilities to the lower grades of postal servants to insure their lives and to popularize the Fund, sanction was obtained to grant to these officials from the Post Office Guarantee Fund travelling expenses actually incurred by them in their journey for examination by the medical officer for insurance, provided the proposer actually took out a policy and paid the premium for not less than twelve months. In 1912 Mr. Ackland, the Actuary at the India Office, made a thorough investigation into the past experience of the Fund from the statistics furnished to him. He drew up a report showing the results of the investigation and prepared fresh tables of mortality statistics, as well as new tables of premia for both Life Insurance and Endowment Assurance. He also prepared new formulæ for the calculation of paid-up policies, surrender values, etc., and recommended the following further concessions and changes :—

(1) The grant to all policy holders on the 31st March, 1912 (the valuation date), of a bonus at the rate of 2 per cent per annum in the case of Whole Life Assurances, and at 1 per cent in the case of Endowment Assurances in respect of each month's premium paid since 31st March, 1907, up to 31st March, 1912.

(2) The grant of an interim bonus at half of the above rates in respect of the premiums paid since 31st March, 1912, in the case of policies which became claims by death or survivance between 1st April, 1912, and 31st March, 1917, provided that premiums have been paid for at least five years and up to date of death or survivance.

(3) "Age next birthday" should be taken as the age at entry for all classes of Assurances.

(4) An integral number of years' premia should be charged on Endowment Assurance policies and Life policies with limited payments.

(5) Transfers from the Whole Life to the Endowment Assurance class or vice versa should be allowed only after any number of complete years' premia have been paid.

(6) When surrender values were granted in the Monthly Allowance class, medical examination at the policy holder's expense should be insisted on and payment should in no case exceed 95 per cent of the present value of the monthly allowance.

(7) Policy holders should be allowed to commute future premia by payment either of a lump sum or of an increased monthly premium ceasing at age 50 or 55.

(8) Transfers from the Endowment Assurance to the Whole Life class should be allowed only on the production of a fresh medical certificate obtained at the policy holder's expense.

(9) The valuations of the Fund should be made at quinquennial intervals.

It was also decided that, as an Actuary had been appointed by the Government of India, all questions relating to the administration of the Fund, as well as future valuations of the Fund, might be dealt with by that officer instead of being submitted to the Secretary of State.

INDEX